The Ultimate
Ultimate Detroit
Tigers Trivia Book

The Ultimate Ultimate Detroit Tigers Trivia Book

A Journey Through Detroit Tiger History By Way of Trivia

Eric J. Pierzchala

iUniverse, Inc.
New York Lincoln Shanghai

The Ultimate Ultimate Detroit Tigers Trivia Book
A Journey Through Detroit Tiger History By Way of Trivia

iUniverse books may be ordered through booksellers or by contacting:

iUniverse
2021 Pine Lake Road, Suite 100
Lincoln, NE 68512
www.iuniverse.com
1-800-Authors (1-800-288-4677)

The views expressed in this work are solely those of the author and do not necessarily reflect the views of the publisher, and the publisher hereby disclaims any responsibility for them.

ISBN-13: 978-0-595-42035-3 (pbk)
ISBN-13: 978-0-595-86380-8 (ebk)
ISBN-10: 0-595-42035-4 (pbk)
ISBN-10: 0-595-86380-9 (ebk)

Printed in the United States of America

Inspiration and Dedication

As I sat underneath the right field upper deck watching the last outs, of the last game ever played at old Tiger Stadium, I began to reminisce about the happiness that Tiger baseball brought to me as a child and how "talking baseball" had introduced me into the world of adult conversation.

Shortly after, with these thoughts of reverie still bouncing through my baseball head, I began to search for a trivia book about my hometown Detroit Tigers. The search brought few results and I found all the choices either dated or not entirely satisfying.

And so, I began to explore the possibility of creating my own Detroit Tigers' trivia book. Question by question, the book began to grow. Over the past six years, I have accumulated questions from reading not only Detroit Tiger history but also major league baseball history. The result of my passion and effort is the book here before you today, *The Ultimate Ultimate Detroit Tigers Trivia Book: A Journey Through Detroit Tiger History By Way of Trivia.*

Written with pride in my hometown team, *The Ultimate Ultimate Detroit Tigers Trivia Book* was meticulously crafted as I looked for trivia, facts, paths, stories, and through the obscure tangents and threads of baseball lore, in order to create, what I hope, is not only the most original Detroit Tiger question and answer book to date, but also a true Tiger treasure that reminds the reader of the Detroit Tigers' very special place in major league baseball history.

I would like to thank my entire family for sparking in me a love for baseball, learning, and literature, for carting me down to that old Stadium down on The Corner, and sometimes even putting me up on their shoulders not only at the ball park, but in life, so that I could more clearly see the game. I would also like to thank all of my dear friends who have continued to be behind my efforts no matter what venture I have undertaken. And of course, I would be remiss if I did not thank that legendary ghost, that mythical creator of this marvelous and magical game that has brought me so much joy and so many opportunities throughout my life and is still the game that continues to be my favorite pastime.

To all of these friends and family I dedicate, *The Ultimate Ultimate Detroit Tigers Trivia Book: A Journey Through Detroit Tiger History By Way of Trivia.*

Contents

Acknowledgments

Sharon Arend: Detroit Tigers' Organization

Joy Elliot: iuniverse publishing

Pat Kelly: Baseball Hall of Fame

Ben McClain: Reader

Helen Pierzchala

Heather Pope: Editor

Michael Tabatowski: Cover Design

The Ultimate Ultimate Detroit Tigers Trivia Book

The great Ty Cobb takes another base by force. In 1909, Cobb became
the only player to win the quadruple crown leading the American
League in Batting Average, Home Runs, RBIs, and Stolen Bases.

National Baseball Hall of Fame Library Cooperstown, N.Y.

First Inning: Tiger Basics

Must-Knows For All Tiger Fans, the Tall and the Small …

1) Considered one of the greatest players of all-time, this Tiger still holds the career major league mark for the highest lifetime batting average at .367, and is second on the all-time hit list with 4,191?

_____

2) This Tiger Hall-of-Famer played all of his 22 seasons in a Tiger uniform, amassing 3,007 hits and 399 home runs?

_____

3) He burst onto the baseball scene in 1976 with a 19-9 record, a league leading 2.34 ERA, and filled Tiger Stadium with summer chants of "Bird! Bird! Bird!"

_____

4) This longtime Tiger favorite hit two home runs into the right field upper deck in Game 5 of the 1984 World Series, the second he hit came off of his hard throwing nemesis Goose Gossage and effectively sealed up the '84 World Championship for the Tigers?

_____

5) This Tiger Hall-of-Famer holds the Tiger single season record with 58 home runs, a mark that he reached in 1938?

_____

6) In 1990, he became the second player to hit 50 home runs in a Tiger uniform, a year after playing in Japan?

_____

7) This portly portsider won three games in the 1968 World Series, including pitching the Tigers to victory in the all-deciding Game 7 against Bob Gibson, to lead the '68 Tigers to their first championship in 23 years.

_____

8) The longtime Tigers' double play combo, they both played their first game on September 9th, 1977, and it was the first of 1,918 games that they played together in Tiger uniform?

_____   and   _____

9) The only pitcher in major league history to win two straight Most Valuable Player Awards, he accomplished the feat with 29 wins in 1944 and then 25 wins in 1945?

_____

10) This Tiger was the last pitcher in the major leagues to win 30 games in a season, in 1968?

_____

11) This left-handed reliever won the American League Cy Young Award and the American League MVP for his outstanding performance during the championship run of 1984?

_____

Bonus Must-Know: Knowledge that every Tiger fan must pass on to their children for the pure magic of the myth …

12) This Tiger outfielder of the late fifties and early sixties, achieved fame for hitting especially well on Sundays. Forty of his career 148 home runs came on Sundays, including a four-homer day on June 14th, 1959, against the hated Yankees in a double-header. His magical productivity, on the day of rest, earned "Paw Paw" the moniker, "Always on Sunday." Can you name that Tiger?

———————————————

Tiger Greats and Their Feats

Now that the easy ones are out of the way, it's time to separate the fair weather fan from the true Tiger faithful. How well do you know our Tiger greats? Find the FALSE STATEMENT among these Tigers' achievements.

Which of the following is the FALSE statement about Ty Cobb?

13) Ty Cobb   _____

A. The only member of the Tigers to be one of the original members elected to the Hall of Fame in 1936, Cobb received the highest percentage of votes ever for an elected Hall-of-Famer.

B. Cobb was the leading vote getter of the original players elected into the Hall of Fame.

C. Cobb won 12 career batting titles.

D. Cobb has the most career steals of home.

Which of these lines about Al Kaline is the only FALSE statement about Kaline's career?

14) Al Kaline   _____

A. Kaline was the only player to face Rocky Colavito in both of the games that Colavito pitched.

B. Kaline put up the most hits by an American League teenager in a single season in 1954, with 139 hits.

C. Kaline was the youngest player to hit a grand slam.

D. Kaline never played one inning in the minor leagues.

Because Jim Bunning's career was almost evenly split between the American League and National League, Bunning was the first to accomplish many pitching feats in both leagues. Which one of these four feats did Jim Bunning NOT accomplish?

15) Jim Bunning   _____

A. Bunning, twice, pitched three perfect innings in an All-Star Game.

B. Bunning was the first pitcher since Cy Young to win over 100 games in both leagues and strike out over 1,000 batters in each league.

C. He pitched a no-hitter for Detroit and later pitched a perfect game for Philadelphia.

D. Bunning won 20 games in both the American and National League.

Who knows what numbers Hank Greenberg might have put up if he hadn't missed parts of four seasons due to World War II. All of these statements are true of Greenberg's career EXCEPT WHICH STATEMENT?

16) Hank Greenberg   _____

A. Greenberg's 183 RBIs in 1937 are the second most in a single American League season.

B. When Greenberg hit 58 home runs in 1938, it was the second highest home run total for a single major league season.

C. Greenberg hit at least one home run in each of the four World Series that he played in.

D. Greenberg led the A.L. in home runs in his last season as a Tiger.

Hall-of-Famers Hank Greenberg and Charlie Gehringer played together in Tiger uniform for 12 seasons. Which of these statements about the G Men is UNTRUE?

17) The G Men   _____

A. Greenberg and Gehringer both drove in 100 runs, seven times.

B. Greenberg and Gehringer both hit 60 doubles in a single season.

C. Both Gehringer and Greenberg played in 155 games in a 154 game single season.

D. Gehringer and Greenberg both represented the Tigers in the first All-Star Game.

Jack Morris had a highly productive and, some may argue, Hall of Fame career. Which of the following did Jack Morris NOT accomplish?

18) Jack Morris   _____

A. Morris was the winningest pitcher of the 1980s.

B. Morris won 15 or more games ten times with the Tigers.

C. Morris won 20 games with three different teams.

D. Morris started 11 Opening Day games for the Tigers.

Sparky Anderson's Hall of Fame career as a manager spanned 26 seasons. Seventeen of those seasons were spent with the Detroit Tigers. Which of these feats did Anderson NOT attain in his managerial career?

19) Sparky Anderson   _____

A. He was the first manager to lead teams in both leagues to World Series Titles and 100-win seasons.

B. Sparky led the Tigers to two 100-win seasons.

C. When he retired, Sparky had accumulated the third most wins of all time, behind Connie Mack and John McGraw.

D. At his retirement, Anderson was the all-time victory leader for both the Cincinnati Reds and the Detroit Tigers.

Up the Middle with Trammell or Whitaker and One Hodge Pudge

On September 9th, 1977, Lou Whitaker and Alan Trammell both played in their major league debut, their first of an A.L. record 1,918 games together, and their statistics eerily paralleled each other throughout their careers. Alan or Lou? Who is the answer?

20) More career hits? _____

21) More career home runs? _____

22) Higher career batting average? _____

23) More career stolen bases? _____

24) More home runs in a single season? _____

25) Most RBIs in a single season? _____

26) Highest batting average in a single season? _____

27) Hits in a single season? _____

28) Tram and Lou played their last game together in 1995. Was it Whitaker or Trammell who continued on in 1996 for one more season? _____

29) Alan Trammell and Lou Whitaker were teammates for a record number of seasons. For how many seasons were Trammell and Whitaker teammates? _____

A. 19   B. 18   C. 17   D. 15

In 2004, the Detroit Tigers signed perhaps their most prolific free-agent in Tiger history, signing future Hall-of-Famer Ivan Rodriguez to a four year, 40 million dollar deal. Which of these statements about our "Pudge" is UNTRUE?

30) Hodge Pudge   _____

A. In 1992, as a 19 year-old, Pudge was the youngest player to appear in the A.L. during his rookie season.

B. Pudge is the holder of more than ten Gold Gloves.

C. Rodriguez was the 1999 A.L. MVP.

D. Pudge was the 2003 N.L.C.S. MVP.

The wind and the pitch ... Mark Fidrych delivers one of his "keep it low" fastballs. During his phenomenal rookie season of 1976, "The Bird" not only ignited Detroit but the nation during a nationally televised June 28th, 5-1 win, over the New York Yankees.

National Baseball Hall of Fame Library Cooperstown, N.Y.

Second Inning: Names, Faces, and Places

Nickname Match

Some of the more interesting nicknames in baseball history came out of the first 50 years of Tiger baseball. Can you match these Tigers with their nicknames?

Nickname Match #1

Ee-Yah   Bucketfoot Al   Schoolboy

Skids   Germany   Slug   Hooks   Piano Legs

The Mechanical Man   The Georgia Peach

1) Harry Heilmann   _____

2) Hughie Jennings   _____

3) Charles Hickman   _____

4) George Dauss   _____

5) Charlie Gehringer   _____

6) Aloysius Simmons   _____

7) Johnny Lipon   _____

8) Ty Cobb   _____

9) Herman Schaefer   _____

10) Lynwood Rowe   _____

Nickname Match #2

Judge   Kangaroo   Rocky   Fats

Rowdy Richard   Boom-Boom

Wild Bill   Baby Doll   The Tabasco Kid   The People's Cherce

11) William Donovan   _____

12) Davy Jones   _____

13) William Jacobson   _____

14) Walter Beck   _____

15) Norman Elberfeld   _____

16) John Stone   _____

17) Fred "Dixie" Walker   _____

18) Ralph Works   _____

19) Dick Bartell   _____

20) Bob Fothergill   _____

Nickname Match #3

	Sheriff	Birdie
Sassafras	Abba Dabba	Dizzy

21) George Tebbetts   _____

22) Del Gainer   _____

23) Jim Tobin   _____

24) Paul Trout   _____

25) George Winter   _____

Bonus Match:

26) Which Tiger was the "Battleship" and which Tiger was the "Sea Lion"?

Ed Gremminger   _____

Charley Hall   _____

Tiger Nicknames Since 1950 Match

Since 1950, the Tigers have continued to house some of the game's more color-ful nicknames. Can you match these Tigers with their more modern nick-names?

Duke   Fire   The Bird   Snake   King Kong

The Earl of Snohomish   The Yankee Killer   The Walking Man

The Sphinx   The Vulture   Footsie

Hurricane   Hot Sauce   Whiplash   Senor Smoke

1) Phil Regan   _____

2) Frank Lary   _____

3) Kevin Saucier   _____

4) Duane Sims   _____

5) Virgil Trucks   _____

6) Don Mossi   _____

7) Charlie Keller   _____

8) Mark Fidrych   _____

9) Earl Torgeson   _____

10) Wayne Belardi   _____

11) Eddie Yost   _____

12) Bob Hazle   _____

13) Aurelio Lopez   _____

14) Julio Navarro   _____

15) Tom Sturdivant   _____

From Parts Unknown

Can you match the Tiger with his exotic birthplace?

Tokyo, Japan   Hollywood, California   Solito, Aruba   Maracay, Venezuela

Waipahu, Hawaii   Santiago, Cuba   Berlin, Germany

Goteborg, Sweden   Tecamachalco, Mexico

Vega Baja, Puerto Rico   Colon, Panama   St. Vito Udine, Italy

Toronto, Ontario, Canada   Willemstad, Curacao   Nizao, Dominican Republic

1) Barbaro Garbey   _____

2) Masao Kida   _____

3) Prince Oana   _____

4) John Hiller   _____

5) Jason Thompson   _____

6) Deivi Cruz   _____

7) Eugene Kingsale   _____

8) Randall Simon   _____

9) Aurelio Lopez   _____

10) Ivan Rodriguez   _____

11) Fritz Buelow   _____

12) Reno Bertoia   _____

13) Ben Oglivie   _____

14) Eric Erickson   _____

15) Carlos Guillen   _____

A Cinderella Story: Ron LeFlore's improbable rise from inmate of Jackson State Prison to Detroit Tiger All-Star was the stuff of, well, the movies. LeVar Burton would star in a 1978 made for TV movie based on the Detroit born Tigers' life called, *One in a Million: The Ron LeFlore Story.*

National Baseball Hall of Fame Library Cooperstown, N.Y.

Homegrown Products

1) This Hamtramck, Michigan native played his last five seasons in Detroit after pitching in parts of 13 seasons with the Cleveland Indians. In Game 4 of the 1948 World Series, the Michigan-born right-hander threw a complete game win to help Cleveland to its last World Series title?

_____

2) This left-hander was picked off of the Detroit sandlots and pitched eight seasons with the Tigers from 1946-1954. Holder of a 59-74 career record, he was selected to the All-Star team in 1950. Notably, this longtime Tiger played for four of the eight American League teams: Chicago, Cleveland, New York and Baltimore, in 1955?

_____

3) Another Detroit sandlot find, this pitcher debuted as a Tiger at 17 years old and played with the Tigers from 1945-1953. With the Tigers, this right-hander suffered through a 2-16 season in 1948, and a 8-20 season in 1952; yet, by the end of his career had nearly evened out his career record at 87-91 with seasons of 15-10 in 1949, 19-12 in 1950, and then a 15-7 record while pitching for the 1954 Cleveland Indians, a team that won 111 games. Who was this "Artful" pitcher?

_____

4) A Detroit native and former University of Michigan defensive end, he made his first appearance as a Tiger in 1961, at the age of 19, and would go on to be an 11-time All-Star in his 15 seasons as a Tiger. When he retired, he held the all-time catcher's mark for putouts and had the highest fielding percentage for a catcher in baseball history. Can you name this Tiger?

_____

5) The 1962 A.L. Rookie of the Year with the Yankees, this Detroit native played in three World Series in pinstripes from 1962-1964, and hit at least one home run in each Fall Classic. He began his career as a shortstop, but moved to the

outfield in his second full year. By the time he joined the Tigers for the last half of his last season, in 1969, he was playing shortstop again. Can you name this nine year major league veteran and 94-game Tiger?

_____

6) This Detroit born, 6' 6", 230 pound "Monster" was perhaps the premier reliever in the American League from his rookie year of 1962, through 1965 when he saved 100 games, won 49 more, and averaged over a strikeout per inning coming out of the bullpen for the Boston Red Sox. He joined the Tigers at the beginning of his last year, in 1969, and put up a 2-2 record in 11 games before being sold to the expansion Montreal Expos?

_____

7) A Detroit native, he was given a try-out out of Jackson State Prison and was signed by the Tigers in 1973. By 1976, he was an All-Star with a 30-game hitting streak to his name. He was traded to Montreal after the 1979 season, and in 1980, he became the first player to lead both the American and National League in stolen bases, having topped the American League in 1978 with 68 steals for the Tigers, and then leading the National League, in 1980, with 97 steals in his first season with Montreal. Need another clue? He's truly "One in a Million."

_____

8) This Grand Rapids native won 15 games for the Tigers in his rookie season of 1977 and spent eight of his ten major league seasons in Detroit as a spot starter and reliever while putting up a respectable 57-46 record with 10 saves. He was also a member of the '84 Tigers?

_____

9) After being named Fireman of the Year in 1976 for going 17-5 with 20 saves for the Minnesota Twins, he was the first player to sign a contract out of major league baseball's initial free agent draft inking a long-term deal with the Boston Red Sox. Boston's investment paid immediate dividends as this right-handed reliever led the league with 31 saves in 1977. A Highland Park,

Michigan, native, he joined the Tigers in 1986 and was 3-6 with 3 saves in 34 games?

_____

10) A Detroit native, he was a hard throwing lefty when he joined the Angels in 1973. In 1975, he led the league in strikeouts to become the only pitcher to win a strikeout title in the American League, other than Nolan Ryan, from 1972 through 1979. By 1980, shoulder problems forced a revamping of his pitching style. Now a soft-tossing control pitcher, he joined the Tigers in mid-1985 and spent seven more seasons with the club. His crowning Tiger moment came on the last day of the season in 1987 when he hurled a 1-0 shutout over the Toronto Blue Jays to clinch the American League East title. After the 1993 season, he retired with the second most strikeouts by an A.L. left-handed pitcher?

_____

11) The 1984 American League Championship Series Most Valuable Player, this former Michigan State football and baseball star joined the Tigers as a highly touted prospect in 1979. Five times in his career, he hit over 20 home runs and stole over 20 bases in a season. He joined the Dodgers in 1988, won the National League MVP, and hit perhaps the most famous World Series home run of all-time when he limped to the plate to hit a game winning home run in Game 1 of the '88 Series. He returned to the Tigers in 1993 and put together three more productive years before calling it quits for good after the '95 season?

_____

Which one of these players in each group of four is the ONLY of these Michigan native major leaguers TO PLAY for the Tigers?

12) _____

      A. Bernie Carbo   B. Mike Squires

      C. Mike Bordick   D. Leon Roberts

13) _____

       A. Ernie Whitt   B. Jim Essian

       C. Bill Nahorodny   D. Clint Hurdle

14) _____

       A. Paul Assenmacher   B. Steve Howe

       C. Greg Cadaret   D. Jim Abbott

15) _____

       A. Bob Buhl   B. Vern Ruhle

       C. Bob Welch   D. Steve McCatty

16) _____

       A. Roger Mason   B. Bob Owchinko

       C. Ken Howell   D. Scott Sanderson

DETROIT TIGERS · 1935 World Champions

The 1935 Detroit Tigers, Our First World Champions.

In 1935, Detroit was the true "City of Champions" with the Detroit Red Wings, the Detroit Lions, and the Detroit Tigers, all reigning as Champions of the World. Here are your 1935, World Champion, Detroit Tigers:

Front Row—Fox, Gehringer, Baker, Cochrane, Perkins, White, Greenberg, Roggins (batboy).

Middle Row—Goslin, Rogell, Owen, Hayworth, Crowder, Auker, Rowe, Clifton.

Back Row—Schuble, Reiber, Carroll (trainer), Hogsett, G. Walker, Sullivan, Bridges, Sorrell.

National Baseball Hall of Fame Library Cooperstown, N.Y.

Third Inning: The Great Seasons (Plus One-Not-So Great Season)

The Great Tiger Team Records

Try to match these great Tiger teams with their number of regular season wins.

A. 98-64   B. 90-64   C. 103-59   D. 101-61

    E. 86-70   F. 104-58   G. 93-58   H. 95-67

1) '61 Tigers   _____

2) '35 Tigers   _____

3) '84 Tigers   _____

4) '68 Tigers   _____

5) '72 Tigers   _____

6) '40 Tigers   _____

7) '87 Tigers   _____

8) '06 Tigers   _____

Bonus:

9) Which one of these eight teams did not go on to post-season play?

_____

1935

1) Which team did the Tigers defeat for their first World Championship in 1935? _____

A. Schoolboy Rowe   B. Elden Auker   C. Tommy Bridges

D. General Crowder   E. Mickey Cochrane

F. Hank Greenberg   G. Goose Goslin

2) In Game 6 of the 1935 World Series, this Tiger outfielder's ninth inning single drove in this Tigers' player-manager from second base with the World Series winning run, giving the Detroit Tigers their first World Series championship? _____ and _____

3) Which pitcher, who had three decisions in the 1935 World Series, one win and two losses, hit .312 during the regular season? _____

4) Who was the winner of 21 games and the A.L. leader in strikeouts in 1935? He also went 2-0 with two complete games in the '35 Series. _____

5) This three-time 20-game winner, won 50 games over the 1932 and '33 seasons, while a member of the Washington Senators. Pitching for the Senators in '33, and then for the Tigers in '34 and '35, he played in the '33, '34, and '35 World Series. He won 16 games for the Tigers in 1935 and threw a complete game win in Game 4 of the Series to put the Tigers up three games to one? _____

6) This Hall-of-Famer hit the only home run for the Tigers in the 1935 World Series after leading the A.L. in home runs with 36, and in RBIs with 170? _____

7) His 18-7 record during the regular season gave this Tiger, nicknamed "Big Six," the best winning percentage for a pitcher in the A.L. that season? _____

1945

In 1940, the Tigers lost the fifth out of their first six World Series, 4 games to 3, to the Cincinnati Reds. But, in 1945, the Tigers began to redeem their past World Series woes. Starting with the '45 Series, the Tigers won the next three World Series in which they appeared. Let's start out with a few questions about the first of the three consecutive Series wins back in 1945.

1) Which team did the Tigers beat in the 1945 World Series? It was this team's last World Series appearance.

_____

A. Doc Cramer   B. Eddie Mayo   C. Roy Cullenbine   D. John McHale

E. Virgil Trucks   F. Rudy York

2) The Tigers did not have a single player hit 20 home runs in 1945. In fact, only the league leader in the American League, Vern Stephens, hit more than 20 home runs that year leading the league with 24. The Tigers did, however, boast the two players who tied for second in the league, with 18 home runs each.

Need some clues?

One Tiger was the Tigers' first baseman and he had led the A.L. in home runs in 1943. The other Tiger played the outfield for both Cleveland and Detroit in 1945; after playing in eight games for Cleveland, he began his second stint with the Tigers after an early season trade?

_____ and _____

3) We Tiger fans, of course, know that Hal Newhouser won the second of his consecutive MVP awards in 1945 by winning 25 games and leading the league in ERA, and strikeouts. But, can you name the Tigers' second baseman to whom *Sporting News Magazine* gave its A.L. MVP Award? _____

4) This owner of 2,705 career hits, he was the Tigers' 1945 center fielder and led all A.L. outfielders in fielding average, while putting up a .275 batting average in this the seventeenth of his 20 major league seasons. The veteran hit a

team leading .379 for the Tigers in the '45 Series and ended his long career playing his last seven seasons in a Detroit uniform? _____

5) He won more games in the 1945 World Series, 1, than he did during the regular season, due to military service which allowed him to only pitch in one regular season game, a game which proved to be a no-decision. No pitcher would again accomplish this rare feat until 1986. Who was this Tiger pitcher that spent a combined 12 seasons with the Tigers over two stints? _____

6) Spent parts of five seasons playing for the Tigers, including 19 games in 1945. In 1957, he became the General Manager of the Tigers and also baseball's then youngest General Manager at 36 years old? _____

Bonus:

7) By 1946, most major leaguers had returned from World War II. Of the eight 1945 Tigers' starting position players, how many '45 starters were the primary starting players during the 1946 season when the Tigers finished in second place with 92 wins? _____

1968

A. Ray Oyler

B. Don Wert

C. Pat Dobson

D. Mayo Smith

E. Mickey Lolich

F. Jim Northrup

G. Willie Horton

H. Dick McAuliffe

I. John Hiller

J. Norm Cash

K. Mickey Stanley

L. Bill Freehan

M. Earl Wilson

1) Who managed the 1968 World Champion Tigers? _____

2) We know that Denny McLain put up a 30-win season in 1968 and that Mickey Lolich won 17 more; but, who had the third highest win total, with 13, on the 1968 Tigers? _____

3) Which Tiger led the league in runs scored and also set a record by playing in 151 games without grounding into a double play? _____

4) Can you name the pitcher who pitched in 47 games, the most for the '68 Tigers? You might better remember him as one of the four pitchers who won 20 games with the 1971 Baltimore Orioles. _____

5) This Tigers' third baseman was only a .200 hitter for the season, but made the All-Star team as a reserve. In his only career All-Star at bat during that '68 Game, he hit a double off of future Hall-of-Famer Tom Seaver? _____

6) This Tiger holds the mark for the lowest batting average for a player with over 1,000 career at bats with a career batting average of just .175. In 1968, he

played in 111 games and hit .135 for the season. Name the '68 Tigers' regular season shortstop. _____

7) Which Tiger outfielder finished the '68 season second in the league in home runs, with 36, fourth in the league in batting by hitting .285, and fourth in RBIs with 85? If you need another clue, his throw to Bill Freehan cut down Lou Brock, who had failed to slide, in Game 5 of the World Series, a play which may have effectively turned the momentum of the series in the Tigers' favor. _____

8) Which two Tigers tied for second on the '68 club with 25 home runs? _____ and _____

9) This Grand Rapids, Michigan, native did not make an error while playing 130 games in the outfield. His defensive prowess, as well as the need for his bat, led Mayo Smith to start him at shortstop in the 1968 World Series? _____

10) In the seventh inning of Game 7 with the score tied 0-0, this longtime Tiger hit the line drive that Curt Flood misjudged, producing a two-run triple to give the Tigers a Game 7 lead that they would not relinquish? _____

11) This '68 Tiger reliever would go on to hold the single season major league save record for ten years when he recorded 38 saves for the 1973 Tigers? _____

12) His only home run in the major leagues came in Game 2 of the 1968 World Series making him the lone player in major league history to homer in the World Series but never in the regular season. Who is this lifetime .110 hitter? Oh, need another clue? He also won three games in the '68 Series. _____

Can you match these '68 Tiger regulars with the team they finished their careers with?

A. Washington Senators   E. Seattle Mariners

B. Montreal Expos   F. Boston Red Sox

C. California Angels   G. San Diego Padres

D. Atlanta Braves   H. Baltimore Orioles

13) Willie Horton   _____

14) Ray Oyler   _____

15) Jim Northrup   _____

16) Dick McAuliffe   _____

17) Don Wert   _____

18) Denny McLain   _____

19) Mickey Lolich   _____

20) Joe Sparma   _____

A trade with the Philadelphia Phillies to balance out the bullpen with a left-handed reliever brought Willie Hernandez and his remarkable '84 season to Detroit. With a 9-3 record, 32 saves, and a 1.92 ERA, Hernandez won both the A.L. MVP and Cy Young Awards in 1984 and helped bring back the World Championship to Detroit after a 16 year absence.

National Baseball Hall of Fame Library Cooperstown, N.Y.

Assembly Line 1984

After the 1968 World Championship, it took another 16 years for the Tigers to build a World Series winner. The '84 Tigers all began with the 1974 draft when the first of the '84-Tigers-to-be was brought into the Tiger system. See if you can match the '84 Tiger to the year and way they became future World Champions.

Jack Morris   Alan Trammell   Kirk Gibson   Lou Whitaker   Chet Lemon

Darrell Evans   Willie Hernandez   Lance Parrish   Larry Herndon

Dan Petry   Doug Bair   John Grubb   Dave Bergman   Milt Wilcox

Aurelio Lopez   Howard Johnson   Marty Castillo   Barbaro Garbey

Glenn Abbott   Tom Brookens   Dave Rozema   Juan Berenguer

Doug Baker   Rusty Kuntz   Sid Monge   Ruppert Jones   Bill Scherrer

Free Agents

1) _____ 1980   2) _____ 1982

3) _____ 1984   4) _____ 1984

Draft

5) _____ 1974   6) _____ 1975

7) _____ 1975

8) _____ 1975   9) _____ 1976

10) _____ 1976   11) _____ 1976

12) _____1978

13) _____ 1978   14) _____ 1979

15) _____ 1982

Trades

16) _____ 1976 From the Chicago Cubs for cash.

17) _____ 1978 From St. Louis for Bob Sykes and Jack Murphy.

18) _____ 1981 From the Chicago White Sox for Steve Kemp.

19) _____ 1981 From San Francisco for Dan Schatzeder and Mike Chris.

20) _____ 1983 From St. Louis for Dave Rucker.

21) _____ 1983 From Texas for Dave Tobik.

22) _____ 1983 From Minnesota for Larry Pashnick.

23) _____ 1983 From Seattle for $100,000.

24) _____ and 25) _____

1984 From Philadelphia for John Wockenfuss and Glenn Wilson.

26) _____ 1984 From San Diego for cash.

27) _____ 1984 From Cincinnati for Carl Willis and cash.

1984

1) This newly signed free agent hit an Opening Day, three-run homer, helping to get the Tigers off to a 16-1 start to the season in '84?

_____

2) Pitched a no-hitter in the fourth game of the year against the Chicago White Sox?

_____

3) Part of the 1975 Oakland A's that saw four pitchers combine on a no-hitter, this '84 Tiger was the second pitcher in this rare feat retiring the California Angels in order in the sixth inning of the four-man no-hitter. In 1984, his last major league season, the control pitcher went 3-4 over 13 games?

_____

4) Only three left-handed pitchers threw for the Tigers during the '84 season. Which one of these '84 Tiger pitchers WAS NOT one of the '84 left-handers?

_____

A. Sid Monge   B. Bill Scherrer

C. Willie Hernandez   D. Carl Willis

5) His sparkling defense at first base saved the first Tiger no-hitter since 1958 and a June 4th, bottom of the tenth inning, seven minute, seven foul ball, at bat that culminated in a game winning three-run homer, captivated a national TV audience and gave the Tigers an important victory against the then gaining, second place, Toronto Blue Jays?

_____

6) Playing five seasons with the Tigers from 1981-1985, he did most of the back-up catching in 1984 and 1985. A .190 lifetime hitter, this Tiger is probably

most remembered for his Game 3, World Series home run while playing third base for the '84 Tigers?

_____

7) Who was the Tigers' only .300 hitter during the '84 season? He also put up the Tigers longest hitting streak that year of 20 games and was the World Series MVP.

_____

8) Who was the only '84 Tiger to hit more than 30 home runs?

_____

9) Only two other players hit 20 or more home runs for the Tigers in '84. Who were they?

_____ and _____

10) Which veteran Tiger, who had pitched in the 1970 World Series for Sparky Anderson with the Cincinnati Reds, put up 17 wins, good for third most on the '84 team?

_____

11) Can you remember the reliever who put up an incredible 10-1 record out of the bullpen and then capped off his nearly perfect season by earning the win in Game 5 of the 1984 World Series?

_____

12) Despite hitting only seven home runs during the season, this outfielder homered in Game 1 of the League Championship Series against the Kansas City Royals, and then in Game 1 of the World Series against the San Diego Padres?

_____

13) His first major league win against the Milwaukee Brewers on Sept.18th, clinched the A.L. East for the '84 Tigers?

_____

14) Spelling the injured Alan Trammell at shortstop in 1984, he hit .185 over 108 at bats. A .175 lifetime hitter, he played in parts of four seasons for the Tigers?

_____

15) Spent his first three seasons with the Tigers and played most of the third base for the '84 team. After the '84 season, he was traded to the Mets, where in 1987, 1989, and 1991 he put up 30 home run, 30 stolen base campaigns and was the N.L. leader with 38 home runs and 117 RBIs in 1991. Name this '84 Tiger who got one World Series at bat?

_____

Where did these '84 Tigers end their major league careers?

A. Atlanta Braves   F. Chicago Cubs

B. Boston Red Sox   G. Toronto Blue Jays

C. California Angles   H. Houston Astros

D. Cleveland Indians   I. Texas Rangers

E. Seattle Mariners

16) Darrell Evans   _____

17) Lance Parrish   _____

18) Aurelio Lopez   _____

19) Ruppert Jones   _____

20) Milt Wilcox   _____

21) Dan Petry   _____

22) Jack Morris   _____

23) Dave Rozema   _____

24) Howard Johnson   _____

And One Not-So-Great Season, 2003

As we know, the 2003 Tigers came perilously close to putting up the worst record in modern baseball history. The Tigers saved themselves from this ignoble infamy by winning three of the last four games of the season against the Minnesota Twins to raise their 2003 record to a 43-119 mark, a mere one victory better than the '62, not-so-Amazin' Mets …

So, although we may have tried to forget, how much do you remember about the 2003 Detroit Tigers, one of the worst teams in major league history?

A. Craig Monroe   B. Dmitri Young   C. Mike Maroth

   D. Steve Avery   E. Alex Sanchez

1) Which Tiger had a team triple crown, leading the Tigers in batting average, home runs, and RBIs? He also led the Tigers in hits, runs, doubles, and triples.

_____

2) After coming over from Milwaukee, which outfielder led the team with 44 stolen bases, good for second place in steals in the A.L.? _____

3) Which Tiger outfielder was second on the team with 23 home runs?

_____

4) Which pitcher led the team with 9 wins? _____

5) Who was the only Tiger pitcher to finish two games over .500? _____

6) How many saves did the co-team leaders, Franklyn German and Chris Mears, have?

_____

A. 13   B. 10   C. 9   D. 5

7) The 2003 Tigers did have a league leader in one category, sacrifice hits, and he was the first Tiger to lead the A.L. in this category since manager Alan Trammell did so in 1983. Which Tiger accomplished the feat? _____

A. Omar Infante   B. Ramon Santiago   C. Carlos Pena   D. Eric Munson

8) Which rare feat did the Tigers accomplish on April 2nd, 2003, in an 8-1 loss against the Minnesota Twins? _____

A. Made five errors in one inning.

B. Had three players strike out four times.

C. Had four pitchers make their major league debut.

D. Grounded into seven double plays.

9) What did Dmitri Young accomplish on May 6th, in a game against Baltimore? _____

A. Hit for the cycle   B. Drove in eight runs

C. Had 15 total bases   D. Hit three home runs

10) Which one of these four Tigers was a member of the 2003 Tigers? _____

A. Curtis Granderson   B. Chris Shelton

C. Rondell White   D. Brandon Inge

Hideo Nomo: The Pause and the Pitch ... In 1995 this "Tornado" of a future Tiger became the first player born in Japan, and having played for the Japanese Leagues, to play in the Major Leagues in 30 years. Nomo's success with the Dodgers, Red Sox, Brewers, and yes, even the Detroit Tigers for one season in 2000, inspired other Japanese players to "slug it out" in the U.S.

National Baseball Hall of Fame Library Cooperstown, N.Y.

Fourth Inning: Go Get 'em Tigers

Thanks for Stopping By: Tigers' Genius Edition

These players played just one season as a Detroit Tiger. Can you link them to their feats?

Babe Herman	Roy Face	Ferris Fain
Wally Schang	Gene Bearden	Elias Sosa
Bill Madlock	Al Simmons	Mike Marshall
Jack Coombs	Hideo Nomo	Sandy Amoros
Francisco Cordero	Hank Borowy	Johnny Podres
Johnny Hopp	Earl Averill	Alex Johnson
Luis Gonzalez	Larry Doby	Steve Avery
Dave Collins	Dean Chance	

1) A former 30-game winner and possessor of a 5-0 record in World Series play, he was the first pitcher to hurl games for both the American League and National League in a World Series. This former Philadelphia Athletic and Brooklyn Dodger finished his major league career pitching his last two major league games for the Tigers in 1920?

_____

2) Hit .284 over his 19 years of catching which included six World Series appearances. He played for the Philadelphia Athletics in 1913 and 1914, for

Boston in their last World Series triumph before 2004, in 1918, and then for the Yankees in the '21, '22, and '23 Series. He caught his last 30 big league games for the 1931 Tigers?

_____

3) This Hall-of-Famer who amassed 2,927 career hits, mostly with the Philadelphia Athletics, hit .327 and drove in 112 runs in his one and only season with the Tigers in 1936?

_____

4) A former Tiger farmhand who was traded away in 1922, he went on to produce a lifetime .324 average in 13 major league seasons. He joined the 1937 Tigers for 17 games, seven years after hitting .393 for the Brooklyn Dodgers?

_____

5) Thirty-four years after his last season in the big leagues, this former Cleveland Indian, and one year Tiger outfielder, was elected by the Veterans' Committee to the Hall of Fame. When he retired, he held the Cleveland Indians' home run record. He was also the first A.L. player to homer in his first big league at bat. His line drive in the 1937 All-Star Game broke Dizzy Dean's toe, an injury that led, prematurely, to the end of Dean's career, and in 1940, he played part-time for the A.L. pennant-winning Tigers?

_____

6) This pitcher got off to a 67-32 start during the War years, from 1942-1945, including a 21-win season in 1945 when he won 10 times for the Yankees and then 11 times for the Cubs, helping the Cubbies to their last World Series. In that World Series, against the Tigers, he put up four decisions going 2-2. The Cubs may have relied too heavily upon this future Tigers' rubberarmed-ness, starting him in Game 5, pitching him in relief for four innings in Game 6, a game in which he picked up the win, and then sending him back out to the mound to start Game 7. Obviously fatigued, he was quickly chased from Game 7 by three straight Tiger singles. After 1945 he pitched for the Cubs, Phillies,

and the Pirates before his last season in the big leagues with the Tigers in 1951, going 2-2 in 26 games?

_____

7) This knuckleballer had a dream rookie season with the 1948 Cleveland Indians. He went 20-7, led the league in ERA, and won the one game playoff for the American League pennant against the Boston Red Sox that gave Cleveland a trip to the '48 Series. He then went on to not give up an earned run over 10 and 2/3 innings of World Series play, earning the win in Game 3 and the save in the Series clinching Game 6, helping the 1948 Indians to their last World Series championship. Never to reach such heights again, he joined the Tigers in 1951, posting a 3-4 record over 37 games?

_____

8) An outfielder-first baseman who played in the '42, '43, and '44 World Series for the St. Louis Cardinals and in the '50 and '51 World Series with the Yankees, he spent his last 42 major league games with the Tigers in 1952?

_____

9) He is probably the least famous American League player who has won consecutive batting titles, and this first baseman accomplished the feat with the 1951 and 1952 Philadelphia A's. During his career he was a five-time All-Star from 1950-1954. He joined the Tigers in 1955 and played in 58 games of the last of his nine big league seasons with Detroit, hitting .264?

_____

10) He broke the American League's color line in 1947, four months after Jackie Robinson had broken major league baseball's color line that same season. He twice led the league in home runs while with Cleveland in '52 and '54, and joined the Tigers for part of his last season in the major leagues in 1959?

_____

11) In the Game 7 shutout that gave the Brooklyn Dodgers their only World Series Championship, this future Tiger made what would prove to be a game-

saving catch when he snagged a Yogi Berra drive down the left field line. He was a Dodger from 1952 until 1960 when he was traded to Detroit in early May. He hit .149 in his last 65 major league games with the Tigers?

_____

12) This portsider veteran of 15 seasons pitched in four World Series while with the Brooklyn/Los Angeles Dodgers, putting up a 4-1 record with a 2.11 ERA. He is perhaps best know for helping Brooklyn to their only World Championship in nine tries when he shut out the Yankees in Game 7 of the 1955 World Series. This pitcher's second to last year in the major leagues, 1967, was spent with the Tigers. He put up a 3-1 record in 21 games?

_____

13) Used as a reliever in his rookie year of 1967, this Adrian, Michigan native went on to pitch for the Los Angeles Dodgers setting a single season mark by pitching in 106 games while gaining the Cy Young Award for the 1974 Dodgers?

_____

14) This forkballing reliever, holds the all-time record for single season relief wins with 18. He also holds the single season winning percentage mark from that same season, with a .947 clip, resulting from his overall 18-1 record. In 1968, his fifteenth big league season, he was sold to the Tigers late in August, but pitched in only two games for the eventual World Champions. Who is this Tiger reliever who also saved three games during the 1960 World Series?

_____

15) A two-time 20-game winner, once with the Los Angeles Angels and once with the Minnesota Twins, this right-hander joined the Tigers for his last 31 major league games in 1971, seven seasons after winning the 1964 American League Cy Young Award?

_____

16) This former A.L. batting champ in 1970 with California spent his 13-year career with eight different teams. His final stop was in Detroit, where he spent his last year in the major leagues with the 1976 Tigers?

_____

17) This right-handed relief pitcher appeared in two games of the 1977 World Series for the L.A. Dodgers. Most notably, he was the second of three different pitchers that Reggie Jackson homered off of in Game 6 of the '77 Series. In his lone Tiger season, he was 3-3 with 4 saves for the '82 Tigers?

_____

18) This outfielder stole 79 bases with the 1980 Cincinnati Reds. He stole 27 in 1986, his only season with the Tigers?

_____

19) A four-time N.L. batting champ in '75 and '76 with the Chicago Cubs, and then in '81 and '83 with Pittsburgh, he joined the '87 Tigers and hit 14 home runs, which included a three home run game on June 28th of that year against Baltimore, to help the Tigers to the A.L. East pennant?

_____

20) In his rookie season of 1995 with the Los Angeles Dodgers, he led the N.L. in strikeouts. In 2001, then with the Boston Red Sox, he led the A.L. in strikeouts. He also threw an N.L. and an A.L. no-hitter, in 1996 against Colorado, and in 2001, against Baltimore. He was a Tiger in 2000 and went 8-12?

_____

21) Played one year in the Tigers' outfield, 1998, and then moved on to the Arizona Diamondbacks, where in 2001, he not only hit 57 home runs during the regular season, but blooped a single off of the dominant Yankee closer, Mariano Rivera, to give Arizona their dramatic come from behind win in the seventh game of the 2001 World Series?

_____

22) After playing his rookie season in Detroit in 1999, this reliever was shipped to the Texas Rangers as part of the trade for Juan Gonzalez. He would go on to an All-Star season in 2004, saving 49 games for the Rangers?

_____

23) Trenton, Michigan born and Taylor, Michigan raised, this left-hander finished his major league career with the Tigers with 19 games and a 2-0 record in 2003. He had been the youngest major league player in 1990, won 18 games twice with the Atlanta Braves in 1991 and 1993, pitched in ten post-season series from 1991 through 1996, and won the N.L.C.S. MVP in 1991. Can you name this Michigan born, one year Tiger?

_____

Unlucky Seven

In an attempt to squeeze past greatness out of these former stars, these aging players joined the Tigers, giving Tiger fans false hope that they might once again accomplish similar feats to those attained before they joined the club.

Match these Tigers to their achievements before becoming a Tiger.

A. Fred Lynn   B. Eric Davis   C. Vince Coleman   D. Gregg Jefferies

E. Ruben Sierra   F. Juan Samuel   G. Juan Gonzalez

1) In 1986, he joined Rickey Henderson, becoming only the second player to have hit at least 20 home runs and stolen 80 bases in a season by hitting 27 home runs and stealing exactly 80 bases. The next season, he put up another amazing campaign with 37 home runs and 50 stolen bases. He also hit a home run in his first World Series at bat in 1990? _____

2) Had a three home run, ten RBI game against the Tigers in his rookie year, and became the first player to win the MVP and Rookie of the Year Awards in the same season. He also hit the first grand slam in All-Star Game history? _____

3) In 1987, became the youngest player since Tony Conigliaro, in 1965, to hit 30 home runs in a season? _____

4) A highly touted New York Mets' prospect, he hit .321 in a 29 game call-up at the end of the 1988 season, bumping former Tiger Howard Johnson from the Mets' playoff line-up? _____

5) His 157 RBIs in 1998 were the most RBIs in the American League since 1949 and he also won two A.L. MVPs? _____

6) He was the only player to reach double digits in doubles, triples, home runs, and steals, in his first four seasons. Set the rookie mark for stolen bases with 72, that was later bested by Vince Coleman in his freshman season? _____

7) Stole 100 or more bases in his first three seasons and was a six-time leader of the N.L. in stolen bases? _____

You Were a Tiger?

Walt Dropo   Gus Zernial   Howard Ehmke   Earl Webb   Johnny Pesky

David Wells   Rip Sewell   Vic Wertz   Phil Regan

Eddie Mathews   Wally Pipp   Billy Pierce   Frank Howard

Jim Slaton   Jack Billingham

1) This first baseman is most noted in baseball history for having a headache, taking a day off, and never getting his job back from Lou Gehrig. His major league debut came as a Tiger in 1913, when he played 12 games with Detroit, two years before becoming a Yankee regular in 1915?

————————————————

2) A .500 career pitcher at 166-166, this former Tiger was an unlikely choice to start Game 1 of the 1929 World Series for the powerful Philadelphia Athletics, who had among their Game 1 choices the league leader in wins, George Earnshaw, and future Hall-of-Famer Lefty Grove. Yet, Connie Mack gave the ball to this side-arming soft-tosser who rewarded his manager's decision by striking out 13 Chicago Cubs to open up the Series, a then World Series strike-out record. He was a Tiger from 1916 through 1922, putting up a 75-75 record during his stay with Detroit?

————————————————

3) This right-hander, known for his eephus pitch, had a five-game stint with the 1932 Tigers. It took him seven more seasons, but in 1939, he became a regular with the Pirates. A 1940 hunting accident in which part of his foot was shot off led to this pitcher's creation of the backspinning slow ball that gave him his baseball fame?

————————————————

4) Despite only a seven-year major league career, this Tiger, for parts of the 1932 and '33 seasons, holds the major league single season record for doubles

with 67. He set the record with the Boston Red Sox in 1931, establishing the high mark for two baggers without the friendly help of Fenway's Green Monster, which wasn't erected until 1934?

_____

5) The Tigers traded this young Detroit-born lefty to the White Sox in 1949 for Aaron Robinson and 10,000 dollars. He went on to pitch 13 years for the Pale Hose where he was a seven-time All-Star. After he had won three games in parts of the 1945 and 1948 seasons with the Tigers, he put up 208 more major league wins to compile a career record, over 18 major league seasons, of 211-169?

_____

6) The only player to lead the league in hits in his first three seasons, he has the right field foul poll named after him to this day at Fenway Park; but, this three-year Tiger may be best remembered in Boston for the play he couldn't make when at shortstop in Game 7 of the 1946 World Series, he failed to relay a throw home which allowed a speeding Enos Slaughter to score the winning run of the Series. Later in his career, he joined the Tigers, playing mostly second base from 1952-1954?

_____

7) This left-handed hitting outfielder spent his first five seasons with the Tigers, putting up RBI totals of 133 in 1949, and then 123 in 1950. He is perhaps most remembered for making one of the most famous outs in baseball history hitting the deep drive to center field that allowed Willie Mays to make "The Catch" in the opener of the 1954 World Series. He returned to the Tigers in 1961, and in 1962 led the American League in pinch hits?

_____

8) In 1950, this 27 year-old first baseman put up one of the all-time great rookie seasons, hitting 34 home runs, batting .322, and tying for the A.L. lead by driving in 144 runs for a Boston team that batted .302 for the season. In 1952, after being traded to the Tigers in June, he strung together a major league record 12 consecutive hits on July 14th and 15th, going 5 for 5 against the Yankees, and then collecting seven more straight hits against Washington in a

double-header. Never matching his incredible rookie numbers again, he came closest in 1952 in the split season with Boston and Detroit, putting up 29 home runs. Nicknamed "Moose," he played from 1952 through 1954 with the Tigers?

_____

9) Powerful right-handed batter nicknamed "Ozark Ike" who led the American League in home runs in 1951 while with the Philadelphia A's. He put up the fourth most home runs in the A.L. in the 1950s, trailing only Mickey Mantle, Yogi Berra, and Larry Doby. He joined the Tigers in 1958, and finished out his career in '59, spending his last two major league seasons primarily as a pinch hitter?

_____

10) Used mostly as a starter while a Tiger, this right-hander was picked up by the Dodgers after two off seasons and turned into a full-time reliever. He promptly went 14-1 with 21 saves, helping the 1966 Dodgers to the World Series?

_____

11) Hall of Fame third baseman who cracked 512 career home runs with the Braves and Tigers. He spent his last two seasons with the Tigers and played in two games in the 1968 World Series. He was also the only player to play for the Braves in Boston, Milwaukee, and Atlanta?

_____

12) This 6'7", 275-pounder, won the Rookie of the Year award in 1960 while playing with the Los Angeles Dodgers. "Hondo" produced 382 career home runs including 48 in 1969 while slugging with the Washington Senators. He came to Tigers in 1972 and finished his career with the Tigers in 1973, playing in 85 games and hitting 12 home runs. He is also one of only four players to hit a home run over the left field roof in Tiger Stadium, a feat which he accomplished on May 18th, 1968, while with the Senators?

_____

13) Upon his retirement, this pitcher was the Milwaukee Brewers' all-time leader in games, starts, wins, innings, strikeouts, and shutouts. After seven seasons with the Brewers, this right-hander joined the Tigers in 1978 and posted a career high win total of 17. He then returned to the Brewers in 1979, signing as a free agent. After five more seasons with the Brewers, he joined California for two and one-half seasons before returning to the Tigers to pitch 22 games in 1986?

_____

14) Over three World Series with the Cincinnati Reds, he put up an 0.36 ERA going 2-0 with 1 save in 7 games. A two-time, 19-game winner, he joined the Tigers in 1978 and won 15 games. In '79 he won 10 more games before wrapping up his 13 year career with Detroit and Boston in 1980. Name that Tiger ...

_____

15) In 2003, this former left-handed reliever-turned-starter, won his 200th game with the New York Yankees. He pitched the 13th perfect game in modern major league history on April 17th, 1998. With the Tigers, from '93 through mid-'95, he went 26-19, including a 10-3 start in '95, before being shipped to the Cincinnati Reds for the stretch drive?

_____

Hank Hammers One: Who knows what type of numbers Hank
Greenberg would have put up if his career had not been interrupted by
military service in World War II. Greenberg won the A.L. MVP in 1940
before enlisting in 1941 in the United States Army Air Forces.
Greenberg then served our country until the summer of 1945.

National Baseball Hall of Fame Library Cooperstown, N.Y.

Fifth Inning: The Good Old Days

The Good Old Days, 1901-1950

1) What was the name of the Park where the Tigers played before the site became the steel-and-cement, Navin Field, in 1912?

_____

2) The Detroit Tigers mounted an unbelievable comeback in their first American League Opening Day in 1901. Down 13-4 going into the bottom of the ninth, the Tigers staged a ten run rally to overtake this team that only lasted in the American League for the 1901 season. What was the name of the club the Tigers mounted their comeback against?

Need a clue?

This club plays in the same city, has the same team moniker, and jumped from the American League to the National League in 1998.

_____

3) What year was Ty Cobb's first year as a Tiger?

_____

A. 1900   B. 1903

C. 1905   D. 1908

4) In which year did the Old English "D" first appear on the Tigers' uniform?

_____

A. 1901   B. 1902

C. 1903   D. 1904

5) What was Jimmy Barrett the first major league player to do while playing for the 1904 Tigers?

_____

A. Make four errors in an inning   B. Hit three home runs in an inning

C. Play all nine positions   D. Play in 162 games

6) The first player to hit four home runs in a National League game, this second baseman accomplished the feat for Boston on May 30th, 1894. He later played for the Tigers from 1904-1907 and managed the team for part of the 1904 season?

_____

A. Germany Schaefer   B. Bobby Lowe

C. Davy Jones   D. Matty McIntyre

7) Which of these players from the 1887 National League Champion Detroit Wolverines, appeared in 8 games for the American League Detroit Tigers in 1906 at the age of 46? Need a clue? In the championship year of 1887, this Hall-of-Famer was also the first National League player to record over 200 hits in a N.L. season with 203.

_____

A. Charlie Bennett   B. Sam Thompson

C. Ned Hanlon   D. Dan Brouthers

8) In what year did the Tigers win their first American League pennant?

_____

9) Hall-of-Famer Sam Crawford played 15 seasons for the Tigers. Crawford is the all-time leader in which offensive category?

_____

10) Sam Crawford was also the first player to accomplish which one of these feats?

_____

A. Lead both the N.L. and A.L. in stolen bases.

B. Steal 100 bases in a season.

C. Lead both the N.L. and A.L. in home runs.

D. Hit 20 home runs in an A.L. season.

11) Detroit lost the 1907 and 1908 World Series to what then powerful National League team?

_____

12) Ty Cobb won the Triple Crown in 1909. We all know that Cobb hit .377 with 107 RBIs to lead the league in those categories, but how many home runs did Cobb have to top the A.L.?

_____

A. 23   B. 15

C. 11   D. 9

13) Detroit lost four games to three in the 1909 World Series to which N.L. club whose marquee player was Hall of Fame shortstop Honus Wagner?

_____

14) Which future Hall-of-Famer managed the Detroit Tigers to those three consecutive World Series appearances from 1907 through 1909?

_____

15) This second baseman hit the first home run at Navin Field in 1912 while playing for the St. Louis Browns. He also led the A.L. in RBIs in 1916 and played for New York and Boston before joining the Tigers for his last two seasons in 1923 and 1924. Can you name that Tiger?

_____

A. Les Burke   B. Del Pratt

C. Frank O'Rourke   D. Fred Haney

16) Which Tiger threw the first no-hitter in Tiger history on his birthday July 4th, 1912? He also had 208 wins as a Tiger, good for the second most in team history.

_____

17) On Opening Day of 1916, this Tiger pitcher collected four hits at the bat, two singles, a double, and a triple, as well as pitching a three-hit shutout over the Chicago White Sox to start the Tigers' season off with a 4-0 victory. Which one of these four 1916 Tigers helped start the season off on the right paw with his great all around play?

_____

A. Harry Coveleski   B. Bernie Boland

C. Bill James   D. George Cunningham

18) In 1920, major league baseball banned the use of the spitball, but allowed pitchers who had made their livelihood with the pitch to continue throwing the "wet one" for that season and then for the remainder of their careers. Three

of the following four "spitballers" were Tigers. Which of these legalized "spit-ballers" was NEVER a Tiger?

_____

A. Doc Ayers   B. Hub "Dutch" Leonard

C. Jack Quinn   D. Clarence Mitchell

19) Which Hall-of-Famer, and holder of a lifetime .342 batting average good for 12th on the all-time list, led the Tigers in home runs for five straight seasons starting in 1921? A fan favorite, he became the first future Hall-of-Famer to be a radio play-by-play announcer serving in that capacity for the Tigers from 1934-1950.

_____

20) Tired of reporters asking him about Babe Ruth's home runs, in 1925, Ty Cobb hit without his well-known split-handed grip and hit how many home runs over two games against the St. Louis Browns to prove to reporters that hitting home runs was nothing special? _____

A. 3   B. 4

C. 5   D. 6

21) In 1926, this 15-year Tiger pitcher retired with 221 wins, the most in club history?

_____

22) In 1930, this Tiger outfielder put up 34 straight games with a base hit which stands as the third best hitting streak in Tiger history, behind Ty Cobb's streaks of 40 and 35 straight games. A hint? His nickname was "Rocky."

_____

A. Liz Funk   B. John Stone

C. Harry Rice   D. Roy Johnson

23) Although not an officially kept statistic until 1969, this pitcher set the major league high with 22 saves in 1926 while with the Washington Senators—a mark which stood for 23 seasons. He pitched for the Tigers from 1933 to 1935?

_____

24) This 16-year Tiger veteran and three-time 20-game winner gave up Babe Ruth's 700th home run in Detroit on July 13th, 1934?

_____

25) The 1934 World Series was the last World Series in which both Series teams had a player-manager at the helm. Frankie Frisch was the manager and second baseman for the St. Louis Cardinals. Who was the Hall of Fame player-manager for the Tigers?

_____

26) In Game 7 of the 1934 World Series, a hard slide by Joe Medwick incited a brawl that led to bottles and other projectiles being thrown at the future Hall-of-Famer by the Tiger faithful. The Tiger fans' actions forced, for his safety, Medwick's removal from the game with the Cardinals far ahead in the seventh and deciding game. Who was the Tiger third baseman into which Medwick had, as Dizzy Dean might say, "slud?"

_____

A. Flea Clifton   B. Marv Owen

C. Cy Perkins   D. Heinie Schuble

27) True or False: Charlie Gehringer is the only player in baseball history to have two 500 consecutive games played streaks?_____

28) Which one of these strange fielding feats did Charlie Gehringer accomplish in 1936?

_____

A. Committed the most errors as a second basemen in the A.L. yet led A.L. second basemen in fielding percentage.

B. Made three errors on one play.

C. Turned an unassisted triple play.

D. Played more games in the outfield, yet led the league in fielding percentage for second basemen.

29) The only player in major league history to hit for the cycle on Opening Day, his 4 for 4 cycle helped start the 1937 season off on a winning foot against the Cleveland Indians? _____

A. Jack Burns   B. Glenn Myatt

C. Gee Walker   D. Chet Laabs

30) In 1937, the Tigers became the only team in baseball history to have four players with 200 hits. One player was the answer to the previous question, and he led the team with 213 hits. Charlie Gehringer had 209 hits and Hank Greenberg had 200. Which one of these 1937 Tigers was the fourth Tiger to have 200 hits in 1937? _____

A. Rudy York   B. Pete Fox

C. Goose Goslin   D. Billy Rogell

31) All true Tiger fans know that Hank Greenberg hit 58 home runs in 1938; but, what was Greenberg's second highest single season total?

_____

A. 41   B. 44

C. 48   D. 50

32) One of two pitchers to win 200 games and yet have an under .500 winning percentage, this right-hander's final career record of 211-222 left him at a .487

clip. He pitched for the Tigers from 1939-1941 putting up a 21-5 record in 1940, but then, true to his career, a 12-20 record in 1941. Over a career that reached into four decades, the Tigers were just one of the nine teams that he pitched for?

_____

33) In 1944, the A.L. MVP, Hal Newhouser won 29 games; but, which other Tiger pitcher won 27 games in 1944 to combine with Newhouser for 56 of their team's 88 wins?

_____

34) True or False: Briggs Stadium was the last American League ballpark to install lights in 1948?

_____

35) The Tigers' 1950 starting outfield all hit .300 or better. Vic Wertz hit .308 in right field, Hoot Evers hit .323 in left. Can you find the center fielder who hit .306 to complete the all .300 hitting outfield? This is a tough one, so here's one to grow on … He played in 15 major league seasons and parts of 11 as a Tiger.

_____

A. Johnny Groth   B. Dick Kryhoski

C. Charlie Keller   D. Don Kolloway

36) Who was the 1950 Tiger Hall-of-Famer who collected 101 RBIs on 8 home runs and was the last player to pick up 100 runners without hitting ten home runs, until Tom Herr accomplished the feat in 1985 for the St. Louis Cardinals? Need another clue? In 1949, this Tiger won the batting title by the slimmest of margins, .00016, to wrest the Triple Crown from Ted Williams.

_____

Lou Brock collides with Bill Freehan and he is ...

OUT!

With the Tigers down three games to one in the '68 World Series and trailing 3-2 in the fifth inning of Game 5, Lou Brock failed to slide on this play at the plate, giving the Tigers a key out which may have turned the tide of the Series in the Tigers' favor.

The Good Old Days, 1951-2006

37) Which two of these Detroit Tigers hit a home run in the 1951 All-Star Game held at Briggs Stadium to commemorate the 250th anniversary of Detroit's founding?

_____ and _____

A. George Kell   B. Larry Doby

C. Vic Wertz   D. Frank Howard

38) Which pitcher, who would be named the Tigers' player-manager in 1952, pitched three innings in the 1951 Mid-Summer Classic?

_____

39) Despite a 5-19 record, this Tiger threw two no-hitters, one against the Washington Senators and one against the New York Yankees, during the 1952 season?

_____

40) He became the youngest batting champ in baseball history, hitting .340 in 1955. No tricks here! Who is this Tiger all-time great?

_____

41) This starting first baseman for the 1958 Tigers was the last player to hit a home run as a New York Giant in 1957. Can you find the former New York Giant and baseball historical footnote who, as a Tiger in 1958, put up 20 home runs?

_____

A. Ray Boone   B. Steve Bilko

C. Dave Philley   D. Gail Harris

42) Frank Lary went undefeated against the A.L. champion New York Yankees in the 1958 season. How many times did he beat the Yankees that year? For his career he was 27-13 against the American League juggernaut earning him the nickname "The Yankee Killer." _____

A. 5   B. 6

C. 7   D. 8

43) In one of the most lopsided trades in baseball history, the Tigers traded this third baseman to Cleveland in April of 1960 for Norm Cash? Cash would go on to club the second most home runs in Tiger history. _____

A. Steve Demeter   B. Eddie Yost

C. Reno Bertoia   D. Jim Finigan

44) In 1960, the Brigg's family scrapped the Old English D for one season putting what on the Tiger home whites?

_____

A. Slanted Script "Tigers" in the Dodgers' style

B. A Growling Tiger

C. Pinstripes

D. Collars to Commemorate 60 Years of Tiger Baseball

45) He led the N.L. in stolen bases in his first three seasons with the Milwaukee Braves from 1953 through 1955, and hit .412 in the 1958 World Series. In 1961, he joined the Tigers and took over the center field duties, helping the Tigers to a 30-game improvement over the previous season. He played with the Tigers until 1964. Can you name this Tiger?

_____

46) The 1961 Tigers had two players hit 40 home runs. Norm Cash hit 41, but which player, in his second year as a Tiger, hit 45 home runs, which, at the time, was the second highest single season total in Tiger history?

_____

47-50) Can you match these longtime Tigers with the year of their first appearance on the big club? Willie Horton, Jim Northrup, Bill Freehan, Dick McAuliffe.

47) 1960 _____

48) 1961 _____

49) 1963 _____

50) 1964 _____

51) In 1962, this lefty thrower led the A.L. in ERA while going 16-8; but, perhaps this pitcher is better remembered by baseball historians for his string of hitting futility. A right-handed batter, this ten-year Tiger was a lifetime .085 hitter, but from 1960-62 put up some unbelievably bad hitting numbers. He was 1 for 28 in 1960, 0 for 9 in '61, and an un-amazing 2 for 75 in his pitching successful 1962 for a combined 3 for 112 over those three seasons—a three-year slump which translated into an .026 batting average. Can you name that Tiger?

_____

52) This Tiger second baseman made the 1964 All-Star team, but hit only .256 in this, his first Tiger season. Perhaps it was remembered that he had played for the Yankees in the '57 and '58 World Series. Can you name this four-year Tiger?

_____

53) In the first game of a double-header on April 30th, 1967, against the Baltimore Orioles, the Tigers won 2-1. What made this victory so unique?

_____.

54) and 55) The 1971 Tigers were the last Tiger team to have two, 20-game winners. The lefty was the last Tiger to strikeout 300 batters in a season, a feat which he accomplished in '71, and the righty won 62 games over a three-year stretch for the Tigers from 1971 to 1973?

54)_____ and 55) _____

56) True or False: In 1972 the Tigers won the A.L. East title by a mere 1½ games over Boston?

_____

57) In the clinching game against Boston in that 1972 pennant race, which winning pitcher singled for the last Tiger hit by a pitcher until inter-league play in 1997?

_____

A. Woodie Fryman   B. Tom Timmermann

C. Chuck Seelbach   D. Fred Scherman

58) The Tigers lost in the A.L. Championship Series in 1972, 3 games to 2, to which A.L. West team that would go on to win that year's World Series?

_____

59) Who was the Tigers' first Designated Hitter on April 7th, 1973?

_____

60) In 1973, John Hiller set a major league record for saves with, _____, a mark that stood until 1983, and in 1974, he set an A.L. record for relief wins with _____?

_____

A. 36 saves and 15 wins   B. 39 saves and 16 wins

C. 38 saves and 17 wins   D. 36 saves and 18 wins

61) The Tigers acquired Nate Colbert for the 1975 season, but his .147 average after 45 games prompted his selling to Montreal. What is Colbert's claim to fame?

_____

A. In a double-header, he hit 5 home runs and drove in 13 runs in one day.

B. Hit two home runs over the left field roof at Tiger Stadium.

C. Twice hit 40 home runs in a season for San Diego.

D. Hit home runs from both sides of the plate in a game, nine times.

62) In 1977, the Tigers had two players reach 100 RBIs. It was the first time that the team had two players reach the century mark in RBIs since 1961. Which two of these Tigers reached 100 ribbies in '77? _____

A. Rusty Staub and Jason Thompson   B. Ben Oglivie and Lance Parrish

C. Ron LeFlore and Steve Kemp   D. Tito Fuentes and Tom Veryzer

63) By the end of his 18 year career, this Tiger, from 1980 to 1982, would play in eight National League Championship Series but would make it to the World Series only once, in 1971, while with the Pittsburgh Pirates. Can you name this Tiger?

_____

64) Lance Parrish set what A.L. record for catchers in a single season in 1982?

_____

A. Most Home Runs in a Season   B. Most Putouts

C. Most Doubles in a Season   D. Most Runners Thrown Out Stealing

65) Larry Herndon joined the Tigers in 1982, and finished second in the A.L. in which category in both the '82 and '83 seasons?

_____

A. Hits

B. Doubles

C. Triples

D. Home Runs

66) In 1983, this Tiger right-hander came within one out, and a Jerry Hairston single, of a perfect game against the Chicago White Sox?

_____

67) True or False: The '84 Tigers did not have a 20-game winner?

_____

68) In 1985, Nelson Simmons became the first Tiger to do what? _____

A. Steal five bases in a game.

B. Hit four consecutive home runs.

C. Hit home runs from both sides of the plate in a game.

D. Have three outfield assists in one inning.

69) Darrell Evans became the oldest player to lead the league in home runs when, at the age of_____, he led the A.L. in home runs in 1985?

_____

A. 37

B. 38

C. 39

D. 40

70) The 1986 Tigers' infield all hit 20 or more home runs. Darrell Evans hit 29, Lance Parrish hit 22, Alan Trammell hit 21, and Lou Whitaker hit 20. Can you

name the Tigers' third baseman who also hit 20 home runs in 1986 to complete the all 20-homer infield?

_____

71) True or False: Kirk Gibson played in his first All-Star Game in 1986?

_____

72) This left-hander joined the Tigers in July of 1986, and pitched in relief for the Bengals through 1987. He had been their adversary as a starter in Game 1 and Game 5 of the 1984 World Series for the San Diego Padres. Can you name this reliever who helped the Tigers to the '87 Division Championship?

_____

73) The Tigers traded minor leaguer John Smoltz to the Braves to acquire this veteran right-hander who proceeded to go 9-0 down the stretch, helping the Tigers to the 1987 A.L. East flag?

_____

74) True or False: Mike Heath played every position except for pitcher during the 1987 season?

_____

75) An Ann Arbor, Michigan, native, he hit the game-winning home run in Game 3 of the 1987 A.L. Championship Series to give the Tigers their only win of the '87 A.L.C.S.?

_____

76) In the '87 A.L.C.S., the Tigers lost 4 games to 1 to which eventual World Series champion?

_____

77) This future Tiger threw a five inning, rain-shortened, perfect game on April 21st, 1984, for the Montreal Expos against the St. Louis Cardinals. Near the end of an injury-plagued career, he joined the Tigers in 1989?

_____

A. Brad Havens   B. Dave Palmer

C. Charles Hudson   D. Edwin Nunez

78) When he was signed by the Tigers for the 1990 season, this outfielder was the Toronto Blue Jays' franchise leader in games, hits, runs, doubles, and stolen bases?

_____

79) In 1990, the Tigers added to their club the first player to hit for the cycle for the Oakland A's. He was a Tiger from 1990 through 1994 and led the A.L. in runs scored for the Tigers in 1992?

_____

80) In 1990, we all know that Cecil Fielder hit 51 home runs, but who had the second highest home run total, with 18, on the team that season?

_____

A. Gary Ward   B. Chet Lemon

C. Lou Whitaker   D. Larry Sheets

81) In 1991, the Tigers helped open up which new stadium with a 16-0 drubbing?

_____

82) This 20-game winner with the Tigers in 1991 set a then rookie record in 1980 by putting up 18 strikeouts in a game with Montreal?

_____

83) In Game 7 of the 1991 World Series, he doubled to lead off the bottom of the tenth inning and scored the Series winning run, breaking up, what had been up until that point, a scoreless tie. Name this Tiger outfielder from 1992 and 1993?

_____

84) On July 28th, 1993, what feat did Travis Fryman become the first Tiger to accomplish since Hoot Evers in 1950, in a 12-7 loss against the Yankees?

_____

A. Hit four home runs   B. Hit for the cycle

C. Hit five doubles   D. Steal home twice

85) All of these Tigers homered from both sides of the plate in one game EXCEPT?

_____

A. Mickey Tettleton   B. Chad Kreuter

C. Raul Casanova   D. Brad Ausmus

86) On May 28th, 1995, in a 14-12 Tigers' loss against the White Sox, the Tigers and Pale Hose combined for a record 12 home runs. The Tigers hit seven of those 12 home runs that day. Cecil Fielder and Kirk Gibson hit two home runs each and Lou Whitaker added one. Which Tiger added the other two home runs in the 12-homer contest, hitting out of the leadoff spot? _____

A. Danny Bautista   B. Chad Curtis

C. John Flaherty   D. Chris Gomez

87) The A.L. Rookie of the Year in 1989 with Baltimore, he joined the Tigers during the 1996 season for 43 relief games?

_____

88) This 1994 A.L. Rookie of the Year joined the Tigers for 1997 and put up his second highest career home run total with, 18 homers?

_____

89) Which Tiger outfielder led the A.L. in stolen bases in 1997?

_____

90) In 1997, Mike Myers set a Tigers' single season mark by appearing in 88 games. In 1998, this mark was equaled by which of these Tiger relievers?

_____

A. Sean Runyan   B. Bryce Florie

C. Doug Brocail   D. Doug Bochtler

91-95) Can you match these All-Stars with the year in which they represented the Tigers?

A. Damion Easley   B. David Wells   C. Justin Thompson

D. Brad Ausmus   E. Travis Fryman

91) 1995 _____

92) 1996 _____

93) 1997 _____

94) 1998 _____

95) 1999 _____

96) When Dean Palmer hit 38 home runs and drove in 100 RBIs for the '99 Tigers, for how many teams had Palmer hit 30 homers and driven in 100 runs?

_____

97) Which pitcher was the starter and winning pitcher in both the last game at Tiger Stadium and the first game at Comerica Park?

_____

98) Which team did the Tigers play in the first Opening Day at Comerica Park?

_____

99) In 2000, he led all A.L. closers with 42 saves? _____

100) On October 1st, 2000, which Tiger became the fourth player to play all nine positions in a major league game? He also went 4 for 5 that day and scored the winning run for the Tigers in the bottom of the ninth inning?

_____

101) On August 8th, 2001, Damion Easley became the first Tiger since George Kell in 1946 to?

_____

A. Get 7 hits in a 9 inning game   B. Get 6 hits in a 9 inning game

C. Total 15 bases in one game   D. Hit 5 doubles in one game

102) On July 2nd, 2002, the Tigers and White Sox again combined to hit 12 home runs in a single game. The Tigers hit six of those home runs in a 17-9 loss. Dmitri Young hit two, Rob Fick hit one, and Damion Easley added another. Which of these two other 2002 Tigers added the other two home runs for Detroit in this second, 12 home run game? _____

A. George Lombard and Wendell Magee B. Ramon Santiago and Jacob Cruz

C. Chris Truby and Randall Simon   D. Mike Rivera and Mitch Melusky

103) If you remember, the 2002 All-Star Game ended in a 7-7 tie. Which Tiger representative went 1-2 in the Mid-Summer Classic and scored the tying run in the eighth inning of the drawn contest?

_____

104) True or False: For the first time in Tigers' history, the Tigers put up consecutive 100 loss seasons in 2002 and 2003? _____

105) In 2004, six major league players put together six hit games, the most players to do so since 1897. Which Tiger was one of the six players to have a six hit game in 2004? _____

A. Alex Sanchez   B. Ivan Rodriguez

C. Eric Munson   D. Carlos Pena

106) In 2004, the Tigers had two players finish in the top ten in batting in the A.L. Ivan Rodriguez hit .334 to finish fourth in the American League, but which Tiger finished sixth in the A.L. to lead all American League shortstops in hitting with a .318 average?

_____

107) In 2005, this durable Tiger played in 160 of the team's 162 games?

_____

A. Craig Monroe   B. Omar Infante

C. Nook Logan   D. Brandon Inge

108) This three-time All-Star first baseman with the Cincinnati Reds was acquired by the Tigers at the 2006 trading deadline?

_____

Jake Wood was the Tigers' first African-American regular, and in his rookie season of 1961, Wood not only led the A.L. in triples but also became the first Tiger since Gee Walker, in 1932, to steal 30 bases in a season.

National Baseball Hall of Fame Library Cooperstown, N.Y.

Sixth Inning: Bless You Boys

Rookie Years: The Hard Ones

A. Chuck Hostetler   B. Sammy Hale   C. Barney McCosky

D. Ed Summers   E. Dale Alexander   F. Dick Wakefield   G. Pat Mullin

1) In his rookie season this Tiger went 24-12 with a 1.64 ERA, an ERA that remains the lowest single season mark for a Tiger, to help the Tigers to the 1908 pennant. Nicknamed "Kickapoo Chief," this right-hander only lasted five major league seasons, reportedly due to rheumatism, but compiled a 68-45 record good for a .602 winning percentage with a lifetime 2.42 ERA? _____

2) Led the A.L. with 17 pinch hits in his rookie season of 1920?

_____

3) This first baseman put up an amazing offensive rookie year in 1929, hitting .343 with 25 home runs, and 137 RBIs, along with 43 doubles and 15 triples, but, his major league career would last only five seasons, due, reportedly, to his poor fielding ability?

_____

4) As a rookie in 1939, this outfielder hit .311, scored 120 runs, and stole 20 bases. His 200 hits and .340 average as a sophomore helped the Tigers to the 1940 pennant. After serving three years in WWII, he returned to the '46 Tigers, but he slumped to a .198 average early in the season and was traded to Philadelphia for future Hall-of-Famer George Kell? _____

5) In 1943, this first year, first baseman, hit .316 leading the league with 200 hits and 38 doubles, and was elected to start in his one and only All-Star Game?

_____

6) This 41-year old rookie played in 90 games in 1944 and hit .298, making him the oldest rookie in MLB history to play in over half of his team's games?

_____

7) This ten-year Tiger outfielder, who hit .345 in his rookie year of 1941, played in 54 games before serving four years in WWII. In 1946, he returned and was an All-Star in both '47 and '48. He spent the remainder of his ten-year Tiger career as a reserve outfielder and as an often used left-handed pinch hitter? Need one more clue? He wore the #6 before Al Kaline. _____

Rookie Years: The Bit Easier Ones

A. Rudy York   B. Matt Nokes   C. Dave Rozema   D. Jake Wood

E. Mike Henneman   F. Harvey Kuenn   G. Glenn Wilson

H. Tony Clark   I. Eric King

8) Set an A.L. record for home runs in a month when, as a rookie, he hit 18 home runs in August of the 1937 season?

_____

9) This 1953 rookie shortstop hit .308 in his rookie season, led the league with 209 hits, and captured the A.L. Rookie of the Year?

_____

10) This 1961 rookie second baseman led the league in triples while stealing 30 bases for the Tigers. He was also the Tigers' first African-American regular?

_____

11) The year after Mark Fidrych took Detroit, this Grand Rapids, Michigan rookie right-hander put up a 15-7 season with a 3.10 ERA. Although never duplicating his performance of 1977, he pitched for the Tigers for eight seasons. His last year wearing the Old English D was the championship year of 1984?

_____

12) This former first round draft pick hit .292 and 12 home runs as a right fielder in 84 games for the 1982 Tigers. After one more season with the Tigers, he would be part of the deal that brought Willie Hernandez from the Philadelphia Phillies?

_____

13) Part of the trade that also brought Matt Nokes to the Tigers, this right-hander put up an 11-4 record in his rookie season with the Tigers, and went 6-0 at Tiger Stadium during his 1986 rookie campaign?

_____

14) In his rookie season, this relief pitcher was 11-3 out of the bullpen, significantly helping the '87 Tigers on their run to the playoffs. He also recorded the lone win in the '87 playoffs, and when he retired after the 1996 season, this side-arming right-hander was the Tigers' all-time save leader with 154 saves?

_____

15) In his first full season, this catcher put up 32 home runs, after never hitting more than 14 home runs in a minor league season, and drove in 87 runs earning a trip to the 1987 All-Star Game?

_____

16) In 1996, this switch hitter led all major league rookies with 27 home runs while playing in only 100 games. He would go on to hit 30 or more home runs in each of the next three seasons?

_____

George Kell: Hall-of-Famer George Kell came to the Tigers in 1946, won a batting title with the Tigers in 1949, hit a home run as a Tiger All-Star in his home park of Briggs Stadium in 1951, and also had a brother who played in the major leagues. After his playing career, Kell would serve as a Tiger play-by-play announcer for 37 years, from 1959 through 1996.

It's All Relative

The Family Names:

Niekro   Boone   Virgil   Perry   Underwood   Sisler   Weaver

Delahanty   Sullivan   Coveleski   Sherry   Kell

Manush   Kennedy   Trout   Nettles   Coleman   Mahler

1) One of five major league brothers, the Tiger brother, Jim, had the second most major league hits in the family with 1,159. From 1909-1912, Jim played mostly second base for the Tigers and nearing the end of his 13 year career, he put up a .339 average in 144 games for the 1911 Bengals. The most famous of his four other major league brothers, Ed, is in the Hall of Fame, but this brother's life ended tragically during the 1903 season. After being suspended by Washington, Ed was put off a train going to New York for being drunk and disorderly, and staggered to his death falling into an open drawbridge while walking down the train tracks. Can you place the surname of these five major league brothers?

_____

2) Called up at the end of 1908 by the Philadelphia Phillies, the elder brother, Harry, beat the Giants three times in five days to earn him the nickname, "The Giant Killer." Harry later became a Tiger from 1914 through 1918, and put up his best major league years with Detroit, compiling three straight 20-win seasons from 1914 through 1916. His younger brother, Stan, went on to a Hall of Fame career with the Cleveland Indians and Washington Senators. While playing in the same league, the brothers made a pact to never pitch against each other, and they never did. They were also the first brothers to both win 20 games in a season when they accomplished the brotherly feat in 1914?

_____

3) The first father-son combination to appear in the World Series, Billy Sr., caught in the 1906 World Series for the Chicago White Sox and Billy Jr. was a part-time catcher in the 1940 World Series for the Tigers against the Reds?

_____

4) A Hall of Fame Tiger from 1923 through 1927 and lifetime .330 hitter, he won his lone batting title on the final day of the 1926 season, going 6 for 9 in a double-header to overtake Babe Ruth. His brother, Frank, had played with the 1908 Philadelphia Athletics?

_____

5) This father and son duo combined for the most career wins by a father and son with 258. Both colorfully nicknamed, the father and Tiger, led the league with 20 wins in 1943, and then was second in the league in victories the following season with 27 wins. His son spent most of his career in Chicago, five seasons with the White Sox and five more with the Cubs?

_____

6) Now probably best know among Detroiters as the longtime Tiger announcer, rather than for his Hall of Fame third base career, this Tigers' brother, Skeeter, played 75 major league games for the 1952 Philadelphia A's?

_____

7) This 16 year veteran played in 69 games for the 1956 Tigers, splitting his time at third base and in the outfield. His son caught for the San Diego Padres against the Tigers in the 1984 World Series?

_____

8) Part of the first father-son-grandson trio, the grandfather played for the Tigers from 1953 to 1958, and was an All-Star third baseman for the Tigs in '54 and '56?

_____

9) The Tigers' first dark-skinned player in 1958, and also the first Dominican to play in the major leagues, he spent parts of three seasons with the Tigers mostly playing third base. His son was a successful catcher with the Phillies and Braves making the All-Star team in 1985 and 1987?

_____

10) This 1960 Tiger pitcher's father was a Hall of Fame first baseman who hit over .400 in 1920 and 1922 for the St. Louis Browns, and also held the record for the most hits in a single season with 257 until 2004. He then sired two major league sons. Dick, the older brother, had an eight-year major league career and played in two World Series, one with the St. Louis Cardinals and the other with the 1950 Philadelphia "Whiz Kid" Phillies. Dave, the younger brother, put up his best of his seven major league seasons in 1960 with the Tigers, where, as a relief pitcher, he went 7-5 with a 2.48 ERA. What is the family name of this Hall of Fame father and these two major league brothers?

_____

11) A Tiger from 1964 to 1967, Larry was part of the last brother battery in major league history. The future Tiger took the mound in 1962 while pitching for the Los Angeles Dodgers, while his brother, Norm, was behind the plate?

_____

12) The only brothers to both win the Cy Young Award, the Tiger brother was the winner of the 1970 Cy Young with the Minnesota Twins. His younger brother was the first to win the award in both leagues in 1972 with Cleveland, and then in 1978, with San Diego. The younger brother was a Tiger in 1973, and put up a 14-13 record?

_____

13) Their 539 combined career wins put them on top of the brother's list. The older, Hall of Fame brother pitched 24 seasons, putting up 318 wins. The younger brother put up 221 wins, most of which came after he was a Tiger from 1970-1972. Who are these brothers?

_____

14) This father and son combined for 194 career wins. Both named Joe, the son pitched for the Tigers from 1971-1976 after coming over in an eight-player deal from the Senators that featured Denny McLain. In his first season as a Tiger, he put up a 20-9 record, and later helped Detroit to the 1972 playoffs with 23 wins?

_____

15) They were the fourth set of brothers to homer in the same game when on September 14th, 1974, the older brother homered for the Yankees and the younger for the Tigers. The older brother is best known as the Yankee third baseman who made four outstanding plays in Game 3 of the 1978 World Series. The older brother also played for the Padres in the '84 World Series against the Tigers. The younger brother spent only that 1974 season with the Tigers, one of his six seasons in the majors?

_____

16) This Tigers' first major league start came against his brother, and he responded by throwing a gem, giving up three hits in 8 1/3 innings, to out-duel his brother Tom, who gave up only six hits that day for the Toronto Blue Jays in the 1-0 Tigers' win. The Tiger brother, Pat, was the number two pick in the nation in 1976. Over parts of four seasons with the Tigers, he put up 13 wins. The older brother pitched 11 seasons for six teams and appeared in the playoffs with three different clubs. Who are these brothers?

_____

17) These were the last brothers to pitch in the same game, for the same team, and they did it while pitching in relief for the Atlanta Braves in 1979. Rick, the right-handed brother would go on to pitch 13 seasons for the Braves, Reds, and Expos. Mickey, the left-handed brother, would go on to pitch for several major league teams, including the Braves, Pirates, Angels, Expos, Rangers, Blue Jays, and yes, the Tigers. He pitched briefly for the Tigers in 1985 going 1-2 in three games?

_____

18) Jeff was called up to the big club in 1999 and was considered the Tigers' staff ace until his trade in 2002 to the Yankees. Despite playing on Tiger teams that were often below .500, he put up 39 wins over his three and one half Tiger seasons. His brother, Jarred, began his career with an amazing 9-0 start with the Los Angeles Angels in 2006?

_____

19) One of these father and son pairs had the longest span between a father and son playing in their first major league games. Need a clue to narrow it down? The senior of the two was a Tiger in 1911, putting up a 7-5 record.

_____

A. Pinky May and Milt May   B. Gus Bell and Buddy Bell

C. Jack Lively and Bud Lively   D. Jo-Jo White and Mike White

20) This Tiger played 12 major league seasons, seven alongside his more famous "Iron" brother in Baltimore. In 1998, he played shortstop, first, second, and third base in his last 27 major leagues games with Detroit?

_____

21) Which of these Tiger pairs are the ONLY ONE of these surnamed pairs that WERE Tiger brothers?

_____

A. Justin and Jason Thompson   B. Tom and Ike Brookens

C. Steve and Doug Baker   D. Milt and Frank Bolling

22) This 2003 Tiger pitcher led the team with two complete games. His father, Mardie, had pitched with the 1978 New York Mets?

_____

23) Which ONE of these four father-son pairs are the Tiger pair? _____

A. Randy and Todd Hundley   B. Steve and Jason Grilli

C. Julian and Stan Javier   D. Yogi and Dale Berra

24) In 2005, the younger brother, Kyle, joined the Tigers for 46 games out of the bullpen, joining his older brother, Jeff, who had thrown 44 games for the Tigers in 2002, in Tigerhood. Can you remember the surname of these Tiger brothers?

_____

25) In 2005, this former Tigers' son, Prince, made his major league debut for the Milwaukee Brewers?

_____

26) What is the name of the younger brother of former Detroit Tiger Dmitri Young, who became only the second, first overall pick in the MLB draft, to homer in his major league debut?

_____

Known as "Captain Hook" for his ready use of the bullpen, Sparky Anderson was a two-time A.L. Manager of the Year with the Tigers in 1984 and 1987. During his 17 years in Detroit, Sparky amassed the most victories by a Tiger manager orchestrating 1,331 wins.

National Baseball Hall of Fame Library Cooperstown, N.Y.

Managerial Insight

Del Baker   Red Rolfe   George Moriarty   Ralph Houk   Jimmie Dykes

Ed Barrow   Billy Martin   George Stallings   Fred Hutchinson

Phil Garner   Buddy Bell   Steve O' Neill   Bucky Harris   Joe Schultz

Joe Gordon   Larry Parrish

1) The Tigers' manager in their inaugural season of 1901, he went on to manage one of the most memorable pennant winners when he guided the 1914 "Miracle Braves" to the pennant?

_____

2) Managed the Tigers in 1903 and for part of 1904. He was elected to the Hall of Fame in 1953, not for his managerial skills, but for his executive acumen. He led Boston to the World Series title in 1918, and began to use Babe Ruth more frequently as a hitter. Let go by Boston after the 1920 season, he was hired by the Yankees as General Manager in 1921, and was, in large part, responsible for assembling the New York Yankee dynasty?

_____

3) Replacing Ty Cobb for the 1927 season, this former Tiger third baseman from 1909-1915 was the first man to hold a major league job as a player, umpire, scout, and manager. He managed the Tigers for the 1927 and 1928 seasons?

_____

4) Manager who led the Tigers to a 1940 pennant and had the Tigers leading the World Series, 3 games to 2, going back to Cincinnati for Game 6?

_____

5) Managed the Tigers to three second-place finishes and a world title in six years of managing the Tigers from 1943-48?

_____

6) A veteran of six World Series while playing third base with the Yankees from 1931 through 1942, he managed the Tigers from 1949 until just before mid-season in 1952?

_____

7) His major league debut took place on the day that Lou Gehrig finally sat down to end his 2,130 consecutive game played streak. This 19 year old pitcher lasted only two-thirds of an inning for the Tigers on that historic day as he gave up an early eight runs to the Yankees, but he would later manage the Tigers from 1952 through 1954?

_____

8) After leading Washington to the pennant in his first two years as a manager, in 1924 and 1925, this Hall of Fame manager went on to serve 29 years in the major leagues accumulating, at the time of his retirement, the third highest win total and the second highest loss total in major league history. He had two stints with the Tigers. For his first shift, the Tigers traded to get this player-manager in 1929. He played in only seven games that season and continued to manage the club until 1933. He was then brought back to Detroit in 1955, where he served the last two years of his managerial career in '55 and '56?

_____

9) This manager was traded by the Tigers for the Cleveland Indians' manager in 1960?

_____

10) This manager was traded to the Tigers from the Cleveland Indians in 1960?

_____

11) Managed the 1972 Tigers to an American League East pennant. In his often quarrelsome career, he managed four different American League clubs to division titles?

_____

12) The manager of the 1969 expansion Seattle Pilots, this manager piloted the Tigers for the final 19 games of 1973?

_____

13) After managing the Yankees to a pennant in his first three seasons at the helm, he never again won a pennant in 18 more years of managing. He is also the only manager to win the World Series in his first two seasons. During his term in Detroit, he managed the Tigers during the dark days of 1974 through 1978, when the team never finished higher than fourth place?

_____

14) This future Tiger manager had 200 hits in 670 at bats for a .299 average, playing for the Texas Rangers in 1979 and is, thus, one of two American League players to reach 200 hits without batting .300 for the season?

_____

15) This Tiger manager is not only one of the few players to hit three grand slams in one week, but is also one of the select few who has hit three home runs in both an American League and National League game?

_____

16) Nicknamed "Scrap Iron," this Tiger manager played 16 seasons, stole over 30 bases three times, and had an incredible post-season for the "We Are Family" World Champion Pittsburgh Pirates in 1979, hitting .417 in the N.L.C.S. and then getting 12 hits in the World Series to bat .500?

_____

These former Tiger players went on to become major league managers. Try to match them up with their terms at the helm.

Johnny Lipon   Jackie Moore   Larry Doby   Eddie Mathews

Frank Howard   Steve Boros   Johnny Pesky   Birdie Tebbetts

17) _____ Oakland A's 1983-'84, San Diego Padres 1986

18) _____ Oakland A's 1984-'86

19) _____ Chicago White Sox 1978

20) _____ San Diego Padres 1981, New York Mets 1983

21) _____ Cleveland Indians 1971

22) _____ Atlanta Braves 1972-'74

23) _____ Boston Red Sox 1963-'64, 1980

24) _____ Cincinnati Reds 1954-'58, Milwaukee Braves '61-'62, Cleveland Indians '63-'66

Try the same with these former Tigers. Match the name to their managerial reign.

Bruce Kimm   Bob Melvin   Chuck Cottier   Ray Knight

    Gene Lamont   Jerry Manuel   Harvey Kuenn   Al Pedrique

25) _____ Milwaukee Brewers 1975, 1982-'83

26) _____ Chicago White Sox 1992-'95, Pittsburgh '97-'00

27) _____ Chicago Cubs 2002

28) _____ Cincinnati Reds 1996-'97

29) _____ Chicago White Sox 1998-2003

30) _____ Seattle Mariners 2003

31) _____ Arizona Diamondbacks 2004

You were a Tiger? Managerial Edition:

32) Spent eight years in the major leagues as an outfielder and first baseman, and spent 52 games, and 53 at bats, with the Tigers in his last season in 1963. He is more famous for his managerial skills leading his teams to six first-place finishes in 18 seasons. In the '80s he led the Cardinals to three World Series and a World Series title in 1982. Can you name this former Tiger?

_____

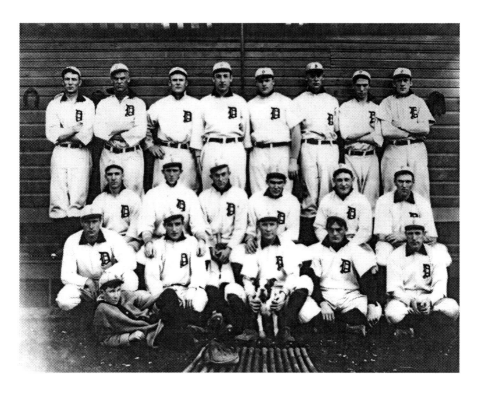

This bunch of scowling ruffians brought Detroit its first A.L. Pennant in 1907. Here are your 1907 Tigers:

Front Row—Siever, Archer, Jennings (manager), Schmidt, O' Leary.

Middle Row—D. Jones, Downs, Cobb, Coughlin, Schaefer, B. Jones.

Back row—Eubank, Rossman, Crawford, Donovan, Mullin, Willett, Payne, Killian.

Seventh Inning: *The Good, The-Not-So Good, The Bad, The Sometimes Ugly, and The Oh So Obscure*

The Replacement Game

1912 Detroit Tigers versus Philadelphia A's

On May 15th, 1912, Ty Cobb is suspended immediately by the A.L. president, Ban Johnson, for charging into the stands after a heckler in New York. The following day, the Tigers react to the suspension by going on strike, which forces manager Hughie Jennings, on May 18th, to field a Tiger team filled out with local Philadelphia amateurs.

The Replacement Tigers

A. Joe Sugden   B. Ed Irvin   C. Aloysius Travers

     D. Deacon McGuire   E. Billy Maharg

1) A former Detroit Wolverine in 1885, and then a Detroit Tiger in 1902 and '03, this catcher appeared in 26 major league seasons, a record until Nolan Ryan played in his 27th season in 1993. While the Real Boys sat out the game in

protest, this Tiger coach got behind the plate for the replacement Tigers and went 1 for 2 that day. Can you name this veteran Tiger?

_____

2) Who was the pitcher who threw a complete game for the Tigers in the Replacement Game, giving up 26 hits and 24 runs?

_____

3) Which replacement player hit two triples in his only major league game?

_____

4) Which 41-year old Tiger coach and former catcher, suited up and played for the first time since 1905, at first base?

_____

5) Who was the only replacement Tiger to play another game in the major leagues?

_____

6) Two of the other replacement players reached base with a walk. One was the shortstop for the day, Pat Maney. The other was an outfielder. Which one of these four 1912 replacement players also reached base?

_____

A. Hap Ward   B. Bill Leinhauser

C. Jim McGarr   D. Dan McGarvey

The 1919 Black Sox

A number of key players in the story of the 1919 Black Sox spent time in a Tiger uniform. Match the crooked, or not so crooked, Tiger to their role in the 1919 World Series fix.

Eddie Cicotte   Billy Maharg   Kid Gleason   "Sleepy" Bill Burns

Fred McMullin   Lefty Williams

Jean "Chauncey" Dubuc   Grover "Slim" Lowdermilk

1) The manager of the Black Sox, he played second base for the Tigers in their inaugural American League season of 1901?

_____

2) This pitcher began his major league career by going 1-1 in three games for the 1905 Tigers. Earlier that season, the Tigers had used this same pitcher, (giving him to the Augusta Tourists of the South Atlantic League), to pay the rent for their use of an Augusta, Georgia field during spring training?

_____

3) An alleged conspirator in the 1919 fix, this replacement Tiger took the field in a Tiger uniform in Philadelphia, while filling in for the striking Tigers who, as we now know from the previous section, decided not to play in protest of Ty Cobb's suspension. This Philadelphia born replacement player played third base and was credited with one official at bat for the Tigers in 1912. In 1916, he became the lone replacement player from the strike game to play again in the major leagues when he appeared in one game with the Philadelphia Phillies?

_____

4) This banned pitcher went 0-3 in the 1919 World Series. He pitched in a combined six games for the Tigers in 1913 and 1914, going 1-4?

_____

5) Played his first major league game with the Tigers at shortstop in 1914. As a utility infielder for the Sox in the 1919 World Series, he went 1 for 2 as a pinch hitter?

_____

6) Pitched in parts of five major league seasons and played his fifth and last season in a Detroit uniform, in 1912. He went 1-4 that year for the Tigers in six games, but, he is perhaps more famous, or infamous, for supposedly being the individual who brought the White Sox and the gamblers together?

_____

7) Not one of the crooked eight, this pitcher went 5-5 in the 1919 season for the White Sox and pitched one inning in the 1919 World Series. He pitched in parts of the 1915 and 1916 seasons with the Tigers?

_____

8) Pitched nine years in the major leagues and was with the Tigers from 1912 through 1916. While in Detroit, this pitcher put up good numbers winning in double figures in all five of his Tiger seasons. By 1919, the right-hander was in the National League, pitching for the Giants. He was banned from baseball for having prior knowledge of the 1919 fix, along with presumably fixing other National League games?

_____

The '27 Tigers: Genius Addition

The '27 Yankees are one of the most mythical teams in baseball history and are often considered, by many baseball historians, to be the greatest team of all-time. The '27 Yankees were the first team in A.L. history to lead all the way from wire to wire, holding first place the entire season, a feat that was not again matched in the American League until the '84 Tigers duplicated the '27 Yankees' feat.

But what about the 1927 Tigers?

The '27 Tigers finished in fourth place, with a respectable 82-71 record, high-lighted by a 13-game winning streak which brought the Tigers into second place for a brief time in late August. But, Our Boys could not catch the Pinstripes, and finished 12 1/2 games back of the great Yankee team.

In other news, for the first time in twenty-two years, the Tigers took to the field without Ty Cobb. Cobb had been named by another former Tiger, Dutch Leonard, as having conspired with Tris Speaker to throw an end of the season Detroit-Cleveland game in 1919, in Detroit's favor, so that the Tigers could pick up third place money. Leonard did not appear at the hearing held by Judge Kenesaw Mountain Landis on the accusation, and Cobb and Speaker, who had quietly retired at the outset of the allegations, were reinstated by Landis and given free agent status.

Cobb signed with the Philadelphia A's to begin his twenty-third season.

1927 also marked the arrival of the first Tiger games to be broadcast by radio with Ty Tyson at the mike, and, let us not forget, that our Tigers did this all without wearing the Old English D. In 1927, a cartoon Tiger head was placed on the Tigers' uniform, taking the place of the Old English D, until 1929, when our favorite "D" was returned to the home whites up until the present day.

So now, with your memory well jogged, how much else do you remember about the 1927 Tigers?

1) Babe Ruth led the league with 60 home runs, and Lou Gehrig led the league with 175 RBIs, but which Tiger led the league with a .398 batting average?

_____

2) This future Hall of Fame second baseman hit over .300 for the first time in his career?

_____

3) True or False: All of us baseball knowledgeables of course know, that the '27 Yankees had six pitchers finish with ten or more wins. Did the '27 Tigers also have six pitchers finish the season with ten or more wins?

_____

4) This part-time first baseman tied for third in the league in stolen bases with 22 steals, tying the A's Ty Cobb and the Yankees' Tony Lazzeri, despite only playing in 79 games. This Tiger, also, is one of the 12 players to turn an unassisted triple play, and he did it to end a game in 1927?

_____

5) Nicknamed "Fats" for his 5' 10", 230 pound, portly swagger, despite his rotundity, he, nonetheless, hit .359 in 1927, good for fourth in the league and two points ahead of the new Athletic, Cobb?

_____

6) The 1927 Yankees' team swept almost every offensive category in the A.L. but the Tigers led the league in this?

_____

A. Runs   B. Doubles

C. Triples   D. Stolen Bases

7) Speaking of the 1927 Yankees, can you name the four 1927 New York Yankee regulars who later appeared in a Tiger uniform?

_____   _____

_____   _____

Special K'ers

At some point during the 1990s, the Tigers penciled into their starting line-up every American League hitter to lead the league in strikeouts from 1986 through 1994, well, except for Bo Jackson who led the American League in strikeouts in 1989, and who saved himself from the following list by never becoming a Tiger.

So, true Tiger fans …

Can you match these Tiger hitters to their strikeout feats?

A. Rob Deer   B. Cecil Fielder   C. Travis Fryman

D. Pete Incaviglia   E. Dean Palmer

1) Set an A.L. mark for K's in a season with 185 strikeouts in 1986 while he was a rookie with the Texas Rangers. His record was bested by one strikeout the following season by another future Tiger, but, true to his strikeout form, this outfielder again tied for the A.L. lead in strikeouts in 1988?

_____

2) Led the A.L in strikeouts in 1987, tied for the league lead in K's in '88, and then led the league again in strikeouts in '91, and '93. His 186 strikeouts in 1987, while he was a member of the Milwaukee Brewers, set an A.L. record for K's?

_____

3) He led the league in 1990 with 182 K's, but also slugged 51 home runs?

_____

4) This Tiger-to-be led the A.L. with 154 K's while with Texas in 1992?

_____

5) In the strike-shortened 1994 season, this Tiger third baseman led the A.L. when he struck out 128 times?

_____

6) In 1996, the Tigers set a then single season team mark by striking out a combined 1,268 times. This record for times struck out was later eclipsed by the Milwaukee Brewers in 2001, but which ONE of these four 1996 Tigers AVOIDED striking out more than 100 times during the '96 season? _____

A. Melvin Nieves   B. Bobby Higginson

C. Mark Lewis   D. Tony Clark

In the L Column

From 1989 to 2003, a span during which the Tigers put up only one over .500 season, Tiger starters led the American League in losses five times. Can you link the losing feat to the Tiger pitcher?

A. Mike Maroth   B. Tim Belcher   C. Mike Moore

      D. Brian Moehler   E. Doyle Alexander

1) Led the A.L. in losses in 2003, and was the first 20-game loser since 1980?

_____

2) A three-time winner of 17 games, he led the A.L. in losses with 18 in his 19th and final major league season of 1989?

_____

3) A seven-year Tiger, his 16 losses led the American League in 1999?

_____

4) In his final major league season of 1995, his 15 losses tied for the A.L. lead?

_____

5) He led the A.L. in losses with 15 in the strike-shortened 1994 season?

_____

The Obscure

1) This Tiger holds the record for the most errors in a season by a catcher, with 41, but also holds the American League record for most assists by a catcher in a season?

_____

A. Oscar Stanage   B. Bill Freehan

C. Brad Ausmus   D. Mickey Cochrane

2) A catcher with the Tigers from 1921-1927, he hit just one home run in 2,319 career at bats over nine major league seasons. That's not to say he was an easy out! This Tiger hit .304 for his career?

_____

A. Larry Woodall   B. Pinky Hargrave

C. Johnny Bassler   D. Gene Desautels

3) A Tiger from 1929-1936 and then again for three games in 1944, this pitcher has the second highest career ERA for a pitcher with over 1,000 innings pitched. Over 1,222 innings pitched, this Tiger had a 5.02 ERA, but, to his credit, had a 1.08 ERA over four games in the '34 and '35 World Series for the Tigers?

_____

A. Chief Hogsett   B. Vern Kennedy

C. Vic Frazier   D. George Gill

4) This reliever appeared in 450 games and batted 63 times, managing only one hit, good, or perhaps bad, for a lifetime batting average of .016. He was a Tiger from 1961-1967, and a Michigan native of Flat Rock?

_____

A. Fred Gladding   B. Orlando Pena

C. Larry Sherry   D. Bob Bruce

5) A Tiger in 1963, and a 13-year veteran, this catcher holds the record for the most consecutive games without being caught stealing. In fact, he was never caught stealing in his entire major league career of 1,206 games. He attempted only one stolen base in his career, late in a game that his Baltimore Orioles were losing badly, and, surprising the opposition with his blazing speed, he swiped second without a throw. So, which one of these four Tiger catchers holds this record for most consecutive games without ever being caught stealing?

_____

A. Mike Roarke   B. Gus Triandos

C. Red Wilson   D. Lou Berberet

6) In Game 2 of the 1972 A.L. Championship Series, Bert Campaneris of the Oakland A's was hit by a pitch, and, in retaliation, heaved his bat at this Tiger pitcher—an act for which Campaneris was suspended for the rest of the Championship Series?

_____

A. Tom Timmermann   B. Woodie Fryman

C. Lerrin LaGrow   D. Fred Scherman

7) Playing parts of 11 seasons in the big leagues, he never hit a home run in his 1,081 at bats. In 1981, this utility infielder joined the Tigers and would appear in 63 homer-less Tiger games during the '81 and '82 seasons?

_____

A. Stan Papi   B. Mick Kelleher

C. Mark DeJohn   D. Mark Wagner

8) In 1982, the Tigers led the A.L. in team ERA and had a league-leading 45 complete games. As a result, in part, of their strong starting pitching, their team bullpen leader that season had only 9 saves. Which Tiger reliever put up those 9 saves in 1982, to lead the bullpen?

_____

A. Kevin Saucier   B. Dave Rucker

C. Dave Tobik   D. Howard Bailey

9) On September 22nd of the 1987 season, the Tigers acquired this pitcher from the Chicago Cubs for a player to be named later. The player to be named later was the exact same pitcher that the Tigers had acquired, and he was returned to the Cubs after the end of the season? _____

A. Nate Snell   B. Bryan Kelly

C. Dickie Noles   D. Morris Madden

10) In May of 1988, this pitcher balked three times in one inning? _____

A. Mike Trujillo   B. Mark Huismann

C. Steve Searcy   D. Don Heinkel

11) In 1996, this winningest pitcher on the staff led the last place Tigers with a mere 7 wins?

_____

A. Omar Olivares   B. Jose Lima

C. Felipe Lira   D. Brian Williams

True or False?

12) Willie Hernandez once batted for the Tigers in a regular season game?

_____

13) Jack Morris once batted for the Tigers in a regular season game?

_____

14) Cecil Fielder stole a base for the Tigers?

_____

15) Al Kaline played third base for the Tigers?

_____

16) Jack Morris scored three runs for the 1983 Tigers?

_____

17) In 1979, a pitch from this former Tiger pitcher fractured this then Kansas City Royals outfielder's jaw. Not forgiven or forgotten, on June 20th, 1980, this normally reserved outfielder, now a Tiger, hit a seemingly harmless groundball to shortstop. What should have been a routine out suddenly turned ugly as, rather than running to first, the revenge seeking Tiger surprisingly charged the pitcher. The Tiger was given a seven-game suspension as a result of his actions, and had criminal charges filed against him by the pitcher. Their feud was resolved on Sept. 1st of that same season, with a handshake at home plate while exchanging line-up cards, but, can you name the former Tiger pitcher and normally reserved Tiger outfielder who were involved in this strange incident?

_____

A. Steve Foucault/Jim Lentine   B. Ed Farmer/Al Cowens

C. Dave Lemanczyk/Jerry Turner   D. Bob Sykes/Lynn Jones

18) In 1985, this Tigers' reserve outfielder went 133 at bats without drawing a walk. In fact, this possessor of a great throwing arm but not much patience, had 214 career major league at bats, hit .229 over six seasons, but walked only one time in his major league career?

_____

A. Mike Laga   B. Alejandro Sanchez

C. Brian Harper   D. Tim Tolman

19) The A.L. leader in times hit by a pitch in 1983, this outfielder was a four-time league leader in hit-by-pitches, also leading the league in HBPs in 1982, his first season with the Tigers, and in 1981 and 1979 while he was with the White Sox?

_____

A. Champ Summers   B. Chet Lemon

C. Jerry Morales   D. Steve Kemp

20) All of these pitchers had an infinite ERA in a Tiger season, EXCEPT FOR?

_____

A. Erik Sabel   B. Julio Navarro

C. Mel Rojas   D. Lino Urdaneta

After slumping so badly in 1983 that he was often booed by the Tiger faithful, Kirk Gibson burst into his prime in 1984. His triumphant celebration of his three-run homer in Game 5 of the '84 World Series, a shot that effectively sealed the World Championship for the Tigers, will forever endear "Gibby" in the hearts of Tiger fans.

National Baseball Hall of Fame Library Cooperstown, N.Y.

Seventh Inning Stretch ... Take Me Out to the Ballgame

Time to take a mental stretch and see if you can remember from which side of the plate these Tigers batted ...

First Basemen

1) Dale Alexander   _____

2) Hank Greenberg   _____

3) Rudy York   _____

4) Norm Cash   _____

5) Jason Thompson   _____

6) Enos Cabell   _____

7) Darrell Evans   _____

8) Cecil Fielder   _____

9) Tony Clark   _____

10) Dmitri Young   _____

11) Carlos Pena   _____

12) Chris Shelton   _____

Second Basemen

13) Germany Schaefer   _____

14) Charlie Gehringer   _____

15) Gerry Priddy _____

16) Frank Bolling _____

17) Jake Wood _____

18) Dick McAuliffe _____

19) Lou Whitaker _____

20) Tony Phillips _____

21) Damion Easley _____

22) Fernando Vina _____

23) Placido Polanco _____

Shortstops

24) Donie Bush _____

25) Billy Rogell _____

26) Johnny Lipon _____

27) Harvey Kuenn _____

28) Chico Fernandez _____

29) Ed Brinkman _____

30) Alan Trammell _____

31) Deivi Cruz _____

32) Shane Halter _____

33) Omar Infante   _____

34) Carlos Guillen   _____

Third Basemen

35) Marv Owen   _____

36) George Kell   _____

37) Ray Boone   _____

38) Don Wert   _____

39) Aurelio Rodriguez   _____

40) Tom Brookens   _____

41) Howard Johnson   _____

42) Travis Fryman   _____

43) Dean Palmer   _____

44) Eric Munson   _____

45) Brandon Inge   _____

Catchers

46) Charles Schmidt   _____

47) Oscar Stanage   _____

48) Johnny Bassler   _____

49) Mickey Cochrane   _____

50) Birdie Tebbetts _____

51) Bob Swift _____

52) Bill Freehan _____

53) Milt May _____

54) Lance Parrish _____

55) Matt Nokes _____

56) Mickey Tettleton _____

57) Brad Ausmus _____

58) Ivan Rodriguez _____

59) Vance Wilson _____

Outfielders

Early Days

60) Sam Crawford _____

61) Ty Cobb _____

62) Bobby Veach _____

63) Harry Heilmann _____

64) Heinie Manush _____

65) Bob Fothergill _____

66) Gee Walker _____

67) Goose Goslin   _____

Middle Ages

68) Hoot Evers   _____

69) Vic Wertz   _____

70) Al Kaline   _____

71) Charlie Maxwell   _____

72) Rocky Colavito   _____

73) Bill Bruton   _____

74) Don Demeter   _____

75) Willie Horton   _____

76) Mickey Stanley   _____

77) Jim Northrup   _____

78) Ron LeFlore   _____

79) Steve Kemp   _____

Modern Age

80) Kirk Gibson   _____

81) Larry Herndon   _____

82) Chet Lemon   _____

83) Gary Pettis   _____

84) Fred Lynn   _____

85) Dan Gladden   _____

86) Rob Deer   _____

87) Bobby Higginson   _____

88) Juan Encarnacion   _____

89) Rondell White   _____

90) Nook Logan   _____

91) Curtis Granderson   _____

92) Craig Monroe   _____

93) Marcus Thames   _____

94) Magglio Ordonez   _____

Pitchers

Came you remember from which side of the mound these notable Tiger pitchers threw?

95) Frank Tanana   _____

96) Jack Morris   _____

97) Willie Hernandez   _____

98) Denny McLain   _____

99) Mickey Lolich   _____

100) John Hiller   _____

101) Hal Newhouser   _____

102) Tommy Bridges   _____

103) George Dauss   _____

104) Schoolboy Rowe   _____

105) Jim Bunning   _____

106) Aurelio Lopez   _____

107) Todd Jones   _____

108) Jeff Weaver   _____

109) Mike Maroth   _____

110) Jeremy Bonderman   _____

111) Kenny Rogers   _____

112) Justin Verlander   _____

113) Fernando Rodney   _____

114) Nate Robertson   _____

115) Joel Zumaya   _____

With The First Pick ...

The Major League Baseball Draft is an inexact science, and, as time has proven, teams with the top pick in the draft can sometimes project and envision greater feats than a player will ever accomplish. Since the draft began in 1965, the Tigers have had five Number One Picks play in the Old English "D." Can you name these five Tigers who were once Number 1?

1) A first pick of the San Diego Padres in 1970, he joined the Tigers for the last of his ten major league seasons in 1982 and '83 mostly as a DH. He hit a career-high 27 home runs with San Francisco in 1979, but never again approached those numbers. He hit 14 homers for the Tigers in 1982?

_____

2) He was the first player taken in the draft by the Seattle Mariners in 1981. Later in his career, while with the powerful Oakland A's, he won 66 games from 1989 through 1992. Signed as a free agent by the Tigers, he spent 1993 through 1995 with the Tigers, putting up a disappointing 29-34 record over those three seasons, and finished his career in 1995 by going 5-15 with a 7.53 ERA?

_____

3) The first player selected overall in 1983 by Minnesota, this pitcher was a three-time 15-game winner with the L.A. Dodgers in '89, Cincinnati in '92, and Kansas City in '96. He spent the '94 season with Detroit, going 7-15?

_____

4) A first overall pick of Houston in 1992, he spent 1995 through 1997 with the Tigers in a part-time role that produced 19 home runs over three seasons. In 2001, he had a career year with the San Diego Padres when he hit 41 home runs?

_____

5) In 1997, he was the first overall pick by the Tigers. In a single season, he jumped from single-A to the major leagues relying on a fastball that could reach over 100 MPH. He was the Tiger Rookie of the Year in 1998, putting up a 5-1 record and averaging a strikeout per inning?

_____

Bean or Beane?

In 1988, the Tigers brought up Billy Beane to give the Tigers, for a time, two beans … Bill Bean and Billy Beane with an "e."

Is the answer to the following questions Bean or Beane?

1) Was Bean or Beane the highly touted California high school player who was drafted in the first round by the New York Mets in 1980?

_____

2) Who, Bean or Beane, was a 4th round pick of the Tigers in 1986?

_____

3) This Bean/Beane had four hits in his first major league game?

_____

4) Which, Bean or Beane, had a higher career batting average?

_____

5) Is it Bean or Beane who became a highly successful General Manager for the Oakland Athletics?

_____

The Last Game at Tiger Stadium

During the final game at Tiger Stadium, the current Tigers donned the uniform numbers of the Tiger greats of the past. Can you match the numbers to both the player who wore the number during his memorable Tiger career, and to the Tiger who wore that number during the last game down at The Corner?

6   21   11   2   5   47   3

1) Brad Ausmus   _____   Bill Freehan

2) Karim Garcia   _____   Al Kaline

3) Damion Easley   _____   Charlie Gehringer

4) Dean Palmer   _____   George Kell

5) Deivi Cruz   _____   Alan Trammell

6) Brian Moehler   _____   Jack Morris

7) Tony Clark   _____   Hank Greenberg

8) What was unique about Gabe Kapler's uniform during the last game at Tiger Stadium?

_____

9) Whose number, 25, was Rob Fick representing when he hit the last home run, a grand slam, at Tiger Stadium?

_____

10) Todd Jones came on to get the last out in Tiger Stadium. What was unique about his number 59?

_____

Gates Brown: "The Gator," the designated Tiger pinch hitter and long-time fan favorite, hit an amazing .370 in 1968 and is also a baseball side note being born on a very historic day in baseball history ...

National Baseball Hall of Fame Library Cooperstown, N.Y.

Eighth Inning: Hodge Podge and Such

The Hodge and the Podge

Darrell Evans	Floyd Giebell
Charlie Gehringer	Rocky Colavito
Ralph Branca	Earl Whitehill
Al Benton	Dick Tracewski
Gates Brown	Jim Curry

1) According to some sources, the youngest player in A.L. history put on a Tiger uniform in 1918. In 1909, at the reported age of 16 years, 6 months, and 12 days, this future Tiger appeared for one game with the Philadelphia Athletics and went 1 for 4. However, despite his precocious debut, the youthful second baseman would go on to play in only ten more major league games. His last five were with the Tigers in 1918?

_____

2) Which Tiger pitcher finished his career with the highest lifetime ERA for a 200-game winner? He had 218 wins and an ERA of 4.36.

_____

3) Future Tiger who was on base when Hank Aaron hit his 715th career home run to pass Babe Ruth?

_____

4) This Tiger great was not one of Carl Hubbell's five consecutive Hall of Fame strikeout victims in the 1934 All-Star Game, singling against Hubbell to lead off the A.L. first?

_____

5) A Tiger in part of the 1953 and 1954 seasons, this pitcher surrendered perhaps the most famous home run in baseball history. In the ninth inning, of the third game, of the playoff for the National League pennant of 1951, this future Tiger was in relief for the Brooklyn Dodgers when he gave up the three-run, "Shot Heard Round the World," home run to Bobby Thompson which allowed the "Giants to Win the Pennant!"?

_____

6) Despite winning only three major league games, he pitched a six-hit shutout against the Cleveland Indians' Bob Feller which clinched the A.L. pennant of 1940?

_____

7) This popular Tiger pinch hitter was born on the same day, May 2nd, 1939, that Lou Gehrig called his 2,130 consecutive game played streak to an end?

_____

8) This Tiger is one of the 15 players to have hit four home runs in a game. He accomplished the feat for Cleveland in 1959?

_____

9) This Tiger is the only pitcher to face both Babe Ruth and Mickey Mantle in a major league game. He faced Ruth in 1934, while pitching with the Philadelphia Athletics and faced Mantle in 1952, while hurling for the Boston Red Sox?

_____

10) This Tiger infielder played second base for the L.A. Dodgers during Sandy Koufax's 15-strikeout game in the 1963 World Series, and came in to play third base for the Tigers against the Cardinals during Bob Gibson's 17-strikeout game in the '68 series. He was later a Tiger coach and 2-0 as the Tigers' interim manager in 1979?

_____

Jim Bunning	Rusty Staub	Bob Cain
Paul Foytak	Jim Delsing	Cesar Gutierrez
Norm Cash	Doug Flynn	Ken Williams
Ike Brown	John Mohardt	Duffy Dyer
Rick Leach	Jack Billingham	Bill Fahey
Phil Mankowski	Schoolboy Rowe	

11) Who has the second most Tiger career home runs?

_____

12) This Tiger was the first pitcher to pitch for both the American and National League All-Star teams?

_____

13) This Tiger was the first player to appear for both leagues in an All-Star Game. A pitcher, he pitched representing the Tigers in 1936, and then pinch hit as a representative of the Philadelphia Phillies in 1947?

_____

14) He was the last player who had played in the Negro Leagues to make the major leagues when he joined the Tigers on June 17th, 1969?

_____

15) On June 21st, 1970, this Tiger shortstop collected seven hits in a 12-inning, 9-8 victory over the Cleveland Indians?

_____

16) Tiger pitcher who walked Bill Veeck's 3 foot, 7 inch, midget Eddie Gaedel, on four straight pitches in the second game of a 1951 double-header against the St. Louis Browns?

_____

17) Can you name the future Tiger outfielder who pinch ran for Gaedel, after his four pitch walk?

_____

18) This Tiger gave up the first of Roger Maris' 61 home runs in 1961?

_____

19) This light hitter, and '85 Tiger, only homered 7 times in his career 3,853 at bats. He was mostly a second baseman during his 11 year career. Along with playing for the Tigers, Mets, Rangers, and Expos, he also played for the '75 and '76 World Championship Cincinnati Reds?

_____

20) This twenty-three year veteran was only the second player, Ty Cobb being the first, to homer as a teenager and then to homer after turning 40. A Tiger from 1976 through 1979, he spent most of his playing time in Detroit in the Designated Hitter role?

_____

21) This former Tiger third baseman is probably best remembered for taking a line shot in the groin while his eyes were in the stands in the classic baseball movie, "The Natural"?

_____

22) Played 11 seasons in the majors, and was a .241 lifetime hitter. A Detroit, Michigan native and left-handed batting catcher, he played with the Tigers from 1981-1983?

_____

23) Played for the 1969 Amazin' Mets going 0-1 as a pinch hitter in the World Series. This lifetime .221 hitter spent the last two of his 14 seasons in the bigs with the Tigers, catching 37 games in 1980 and 2 more in 1981?

_____

24) While with the Reds, this Tiger-to-be gave up Hank Aaron's 714th home run?

_____

25) This Tiger was a Notre Dame college teammate of George Gipp from 1918 to 1920?

_____

26) This Tiger outfielder was a Stanford college teammate of John Elway?

_____

27) Before being drafted by the Tigers, he was a quarterback at the University of Michigan?

_____

Trade Bait

Ownie Carroll   Dick Littlefield   Doyle Alexander   Juan Encarnacion

Jeff Weaver   Dave Engle   Brad Ausmus   Dave LaPoint

Steve Demeter   Harvey Kuenn   Denny McLain

Frank Catalanotto   Barney McCosky   Kyle Farnsworth   Tuck Stainback

1) This future Tiger was part of a deal that brought Frank Robinson to the Dodgers in 1971?

_____

2) Who was the one-time Tiger that was traded in an attempt to bring Jackie Robinson to the New York Giants?

_____

3) A future Tiger catcher who was part of the deal that brought Rod Carew to California in 1979?

_____

4) This career 65-game winner spent parts of five years with the Tigers, and, during his career, was part of trades for Hall-of-Famers Waite Hoyt, Jim Bottomley, and Dazzy Vance?

_____

5) Post-Tiger career, he was traded for future Hall-of-Famer Orlando Cepeda?

_____

6) This two-year Tiger was the position player included with two pitchers and, more importantly perhaps, 185,000 dollars, when the Cubs obtained Dizzy Dean in 1938?

_____

7) The player traded for Rocky Colavito, a trade that Indian fans curse to this day?

_____

8) This Tiger was traded to the Philadelphia Athletics in 1946 for George Kell?

_____

9) This Tiger was traded to the Cleveland Indians in 1960 for Norm Cash?

_____

10) This future Tiger was part of the six-player deal that brought 1981 Cy Young Award winner, Rollie Fingers, and 1982 Cy Young Award winner, Pete Vuckovich, to the Milwaukee Brewers?

_____

11) This future Gold Glove catcher was traded twice by the Tigers to the Houston Astros, first in 1996, and then again, in 2000?

_____

12) This player was one of the five Tigers shipped to Texas for Juan Gonzalez?

_____

13) This outfielder was traded to the Reds for Tiger fan favorite, Dmitri Young?

_____

14) In the three-team trade that netted the Tigers Carlos Pena, Franklyn German, and Jeremy Bonderman, which Tiger pitcher was the key to the deal?

_____

15) At the trading deadline in 2005, the Tigers used this hard throwing reliever to obtain Zach Miner and Roman Colon from the Braves?

_____

Portrait of Young Tiger: This young man would go on to play the most games in a Tiger uniform, 2,834, over his 22 Tiger seasons, ten in which he would win a Gold Glove.

Simply Golden Gloves

The Gold Glove Award was initiated in 1957 and was, at its inception, given to the best defensive player at each position out of both leagues. In 1958, the award was split to reward the best position players in both the American and National League.

Al Kaline was the Tigers' top Golden Glove winner, winning ten Gold Gloves as a Tiger starting in 1957 and winning his last in 1967.

Do you know the other Tiger Gold Glove winners?

1) From 1957 until 1980, there were only four pitchers who won the Gold Glove Award in the American League. Bobby Shantz won the award from 1957-1960 for the New York Yankees. Jim Kaat won the Gold Glove Award an incredible 16 years in a row with 14 of those awards coming in the American League from 1962-1975. With Kaat gone to Philadelphia in 1976, future Hall-of-Famer Jim Palmer of the Baltimore Orioles took over the award from 1976-1979.

That leaves only 1961.

Which Tiger pitcher won the award in 1961 to be one of the only four pitchers to win an American League Gold Glove in the first 23 years of its existence?

_____

2) Mickey Stanley won the first of his four Gold Gloves in? _____

A. 1965   B. 1967

C. 1968   D. 1969

3) This longtime Tiger catcher holds the all-time best fielding percentage for a catcher and won five Gold Gloves in his career?

_____

4) The 1972 American League East winning Tigers had a Gold Glove shortstop. Can you name the shortstop that set a then record for shortstops by playing in 72 consecutive games without an error?

_____

5) Which of these Tigers won a Gold Glove in 1976? _____

A. Rusty Staub   B. Ron LeFlore

C. Aurelio Rodriguez   D. Milt May

6) Which of these four popular Tigers was the first to win a Gold Glove?

_____

A. Alan Trammell   B. Lou Whitaker

C. Lance Parrish   D. Jack Morris

7) This six-time Gold Glove winning outfielder from 1980 though 1985, joined the Tigers in 1988?

_____

8) Who was the last Tiger to win a Gold Glove before Ivan Rodriguez won his 11th Gold Glove in 2004? A hint: He was the Tigers' center fielder in 1988 and 1989.

_____

Cecil Fielder: "Big Daddy" came to the Tigers after slugging 38 home runs for the Hanshin Tigers in Japan's Central League in 1989. In 1990, Fielder became the first A.L. player since Roger Maris, in 1961, to hit 50 or more home runs.

National Baseball Hall of Fame Library Cooperstown, N.Y.

Ninth Inning: In For the Save

Over the Roof

One of the truly great and memorable aspects about our old Stadium down on The Corner was that, every once in a while, a true power hitter could really get a hold of one and send it soaring out and over roof of Tiger Stadium. How much do you know about the Tigers who hit one, literally, out of the park?

1) Who was the first Tiger to hit a home run out of old Tiger Stadium and also, by knocking it over the roof four times, accomplished the feat more than any other player?

_____

2) Which Tiger homered over the roof three times and is the only Tiger to hit one out of the park in two different decades?

_____

3) Who was the only player in Tiger history to hit a homer over the left field roof while in a Tiger uniform?

_____

4) Which Tiger homered over the roof during the 1984 season?

_____

5) All of the following four Tigers hit home runs out of Tiger Stadium. Three of the four accomplished the feat twice. Can you pick out the powerful Tiger that accomplished the feat only once? _____

A. Tony Clark   B. Mickey Tettleton

C. Jim Northrup   D. Jason Thompson

6) All of these Tigers, EXCEPT ONE, hit a home run out of Tiger Stadium. Which of these powerful Tigers DID NOT get one out of Tiger Stadium?

_____

A. Lou Whitaker   B. Willie Horton

C. Chad Kreuter   D. Melvin Nieves

7) Who was the last Tiger to homer over the roof at Tiger Stadium?

_____

A. Karim Garcia   B. Gabe Kapler

C. Jose Macias   D. Gabe Alvarez

The Rest of the Story

Take this list of Tigers and use their names to complete the story of some of the almost great seasons in Tiger history.

Ty Cobb	Sam Crawford	Al Kaline
Hooks Dauss	Jack Morris	Darrell Evans
Bobby Veach	Elden Auker	Mickey Tettleton
John Doherty	Gary Pettis	Jeff Robinson
Steve Kemp	Mike Henneman	Harry Heilmann
Marv Owen	Rudy York	Alan Trammell
Roxie Lawson	Charlie Gehringer	Lance Parrish
Earl Wilson	Billy Rogell	Cecil Fielder
Harry Coveleski	Herm Pillette	Mickey Cochrane
Kirk Gibson	Hank Greenberg	

1915

For the first time in their history, the Tigers won 100 games, but were beaten out by 2 ½ games by the Bostons who had a young lefty in his first full season named Ruth. The Tigers' offense was led by the outfield where 1)_____ hit .369, to lead the league, and also set an American League record with 96 stolen bases that stood until 1980. 2)_____ and 3)_____ tied for the A.L. lead in RBIs with 112. 4)_____ pitched in 50 games winning 22, and 5)_____ won 24 games en route to becoming the all-time Tigers' leader in wins.

1923

Under the leadership of player-manager Ty Cobb, the Tigers finished a distant second, 16 games behind the New York Yankees. The Tigers hit .300 as a team, but that was only the league's second-best team average with third place Cleveland hitting .301. 6)_____ led the offense, putting up a .403 average and was the last Tiger to hit .400 for a season. He also added 18 home runs which was good for third behind Babe Ruth, and Ken Williams of the St. Louis Browns. Manager, Cobb, hit .340 and seven regulars hit over .300. The pitching staff was led by Hooks Dauss and his 21 wins, the last of his three 20-win seasons. The Tigers also had the league leader in losses, 7)_____, who went 14-19 this year after a 19-12 rookie year in 1922.

1937

On May 25th, player-manager 8)_____ was accidentally hit in the head by a pitched ball that prematurely ended his Hall of Fame playing career. Despite the loss of their manager, the Tigers went on to win 89 games, finishing a distant second to the New York Yankees. Sporting the second highest A.L. team ERA of 4.87, the Tigers won with their strength at bat, hitting .292 as a team to lead the American League. 9)_____ put up his 183 RBI season this year good for the third highest single season total of all time. Second baseman, 10)_____, led the league with a .371 average and won the A.L. MVP. 11)_____ added 35 home runs in his rookie season and hit 18 in August alone to break Babe Ruth's record for home runs in a single month. The MVP second baseman, the shortstop 12)_____, and third baseman 13)_____, all led the A.L. in fielding at their positions. The Tigers were led in wins by 14)_____ who put up an 18-7 record, despite a 5.26 ERA, and by 15)_____, who added 17 wins with a team-leading 3.88 ERA.

1967

In one of the most memorable pennant races to date, four teams, Detroit, Chicago, Boston, and Minnesota, were vying for the pennant, going into the final weekend of the season. The Tigers, forced by weather into two doubleheaders against the California Angels on the last two days of the season, needed to sweep all four games to assure themselves a trip to the World Series. But, with a depleted pitching staff, the Tigers were only able to manage two wins in those final four games and finished at 91 wins, tying the Tigers for second place in the four-way pennant race. The Tigers' strong pitching staff was led by 16)_____ and his A.L. leading 22 wins. Their team batting average was mere .243, but in the pitcher-friendly era, was good enough for second in the league. 17)_____ led the way on offense with his .308 average which placed him third in the A.L. and his 25 home runs which tied him for the fourth highest total in the A.L. for the '67 season.

1981

The Tigers finished the season with the second most wins in the A.L. and went into the last weekend of the season with a chance to make the divisional play-offs as the second half A.L. East champions of the strike-shortened split season. But, our youthful Tigers were unable to win the necessary two out of three games and instead watched the Milwaukee Brewers celebrate. The team leader in home runs, 18) _____, had a mere 10. 19) _____ led the team with 49 RBIs and was traded after the season for longtime Tiger center fielder Chet Lemon. The team leader in wins, 20) _____, had 14 which was good enough to tie for the A.L. lead with three other pitchers. Second year outfielder, 21) _____, led the second half charge batting .328 for the season.

1988

Although the Tigers led the A.L. East longer than any other division rival, a late season 4-19 swoon led to a second place finish one game behind Boston. 22) _____led the team with a .311 average and also led the team with 69 RBIs. 23) _____ hit 22 home runs to lead the club and also hit his 400th career home run in this, his last Tiger season. Newly acquired outfielder, 24) _____, played Gold Glove center field and, despite hitting only .210 for the season, stole 44 bases to finish second in bases stolen in the A.L. Jack Morris led the staff with 15 wins and a surprising, second year Tiger, 25) _____, started 23 games going 13-6, and allowed the least hits per nine innings in Tiger history. Another second year Tiger, 26) _____, also had a spectacular year out of the pen, winning 9 games and saving 22, with a 1.87 ERA.

1993

In what would be the last winning season at Tiger Stadium, the Tigers resided in first place until June, but finished in fourth place in the A.L. East with a record of 85-77. The team scored the most runs in the American League and hit the second most home runs, but the free-swinging offense also led the A.L. in strikeouts. The offensive attack was led by 27) _____, with his 30 homers and his 117 RBIs, good for fifth in the A.L. after he had led the junior circuit in RBIs for three straight seasons. 28) _____ led the team in home runs with 32. 29) _____ led the struggling, high ERA pitching staff with 14 wins, and Mike Henneman led the Tigers out of the pen with 24 saves.

Four For 2004

1) Which Tiger first baseman led the '04 team in home runs, with 27?

_____

2) Which first year Tiger led the '04 team in RBIs, with 97?

_____

3) Which Tiger lefty led the pitching staff in wins, with 12?

_____

4) The Tigers' leader in saves in 2004, he had saved 40 games in both the N.L. and A.L., saving 41 with Montreal in 1999, and 40 with Boston in 2000?

_____

Five For 2005

1) This 2005 Tiger was a four-time All-Star with the Chicago White Sox. While with the Sox, he hit over 30 home runs and drove in over 100 runs in each season from 1999 through 2002 which included a 38 homer and 135 RBI season in 2002, an RBI total good for second most in the A.L. that season?

_____

2) This 2005 Tiger was a four-time All-Star with the Anaheim Angels, and he earned 30 or more saves in eight of his ten major league seasons. In 2002, he put up seven post-season saves, helping the Anaheim Angels to the 2002 World Championship?

_____

3) This Tiger homered three times on Opening Day, becoming the third major leaguer to do so?

_____

4) He won his second consecutive Gold Glove Award as a Tiger in 2005?

_____

5) This second baseman, obtained in a trade from the Philadelphia Phillies, hit .338 over 86 games with the Tigers to finish with a combined A.L. and N.L. batting average of .331—the second highest batting average in the major leagues for 2005?

_____

Six for 2006

1) This veteran left-hander, and the first lefty to hurl a perfect game in the American League, joined the Tigers as a free agent in 2006, won his 200th career game in June, and then took the mound to start the 2006 All-Star Game for the A.L.?

_____

2) Traded away in 2001 to Minnesota, this Tigers' closer returned in 2006 and became the Tigers' all-time save leader, passing Mike Henneman?

_____

3) Hit 9 home runs in the Tigers' first 13 games becoming the fastest American League player to hit 9 home runs in a season and became the fourth player in major league history to hit 9 home runs in his team's first 13 games?

_____

4) In 2006, this one-time second pick overall, became the first Tiger rookie to win 17 games since Mark Fidrych in 1976?

_____

5) A two-time Manager of the Year and manager of the 1997 World Championship Florida Marlins, in his first season at the helm, he led the Tigers to an incredible turnaround, the best record in baseball at the All-Star break, and to the Tigers' first play-off appearance in 19 years?

_____

6) He became the tenth Tiger to hit for the cycle on August 1st, 2006, in a game against the Tampa Bay Devil Rays? _____

A. Brent Clevlen   B. Placido Polanco

C. Carlos Guillen   D. Sean Casey

The Keystone: Playing a record 1,918 games together in Tiger uniform, Alan Trammell and Lou Whitaker will forever be inseparable in the minds and hearts of Tiger fans.

National Baseball Hall of Fame Library Cooperstown, N.Y.

Tenth Inning: Extra Innings

One of These Things …

If you have played all nine innings of this book, you must truly be a Tiger expert by now … so, find the ONLY player in each group of four that did NOT play for the Tigers.

One of these things it not like the others …

They should stick out like a sore paw.

1) _____

A. Matt Batts   B. Charlie Spikes

C. Neal Ball   D. Bruce Fields

2) _____

A. Champ Summers   B. Milt May

C. Slicker Parks   D. Jack Spring

3) _____

A. Frank House   B. Skeeter Barnes

C. Joe Hall   D. Phil Roof

4) _____

A. Eddie Lake   B. Charles Hudson

C. Marcus Thames   D. Mickey Rivers

5) _____

A. Fritz Fisher   B. Dizzy Trout

C. Chico Salmon   D. Woodie Fryman

6) _____

A. Shawn Hare   B. Dean Crow

C. Doug Bird   D. Terry Fox

7) _____

A. Ben Flowers   B. Mike Ivie

C. Les Moss   D. John Stone

8) _____

A. Joe Black   B. Ted Gray

C. Lu Blue   D. Chris Brown

9) _____

A. Ollie Brown   B. Dick Brown

C. Ike Brown   D. Darrell Brown

10) _____

A. Hal White   B. Frank White

C. Rondell White   D. Derrick White

11) _____

A. Luis Polonia   B. Franklyn German

C. Gil English   D. Larry French

12) _____

A. Mel Queen   B. Charlie King

C. Scottie Earl   D. Jeff Kaiser

13) _____

A. Lenny Green   B. Don Money

C. Jim Price   D. Felipe Lira

14) _____

A. Norm Cash   B. John Knox

C. Charlie Silvera   D. Purnal Goldy

15) _____

A. Charlie Deal   B. John Gamble

C. Dave Cash   D. Kevin Ritz

16) _____

A. Dalton Jones   B. Lynn Jones

C. Davy Jones   D. Nippy Jones

17) _____

A. Ryan Jackson   B. Travis Jackson

C. Damian Jackson   D. Ron Jackson

18) _____

A. Clay Smith   B. Willie Smith

C. Dave Smith   D. Jason Smith

19) _____

A. Billy Pierce   B. Glenn Wilson

C. Charlie Harding   D. Reggie Cleveland

20) _____

A. Joe Bush   B. Jack Hamilton

C. Joe Hoover   D. Bob Adams

21) _____

A. Bob Kennedy   B. Otis Nixon

C. Scotti Madison   D. Tony Taylor

22) _____

A. Fred Hatfield   B. Davey Crockett

C. Benny McCoy   D. Alex Burr

23) _____

A. Don Lee   B. Mudcat Grant

C. Marlin Stuart   D. Sheldon Burnside

24) _____

A. Sammy Hale   B. Dan Ford

C. Shannon Penn   D. Charlie O'Leary

25) _____

A. Ed Hemingway   B. Dick Marlowe

C. Les Fleming   D. Ozzie Virgil

26) _____

A. Ray Hayworth   B. George Burns

C. Buck Freeman   D. Leon Roberts

27) _____

A. Al Greene   B. Tom Jones

C. Bobby Brown   D. Jim Morrison

28) _____

A. Gerry Moses   B. Ira Thomas

C. Jose Pagan   D. Bob Christian

29) _____

A. Razor Shines   B. Ted Power

C. Steve Sparks   D. Ron Tingley

30) _____

A. George Thomas   B. Mike Chris

C. Dwayne Henry   D. Dick Allen

31) _____

A. Jim Ray   B. Emil Yde

C. Bill Lee   D. Charlie Lau

32) _____

A. Ed Mierkowicz   B. Doug Gwosdz

C. Wayne Krenchicki   D. Hiram Bocachica

33) _____

A. Dave Wickersham   B. Boots Poffenberger

C. Bill Monbouquette   D. Win Remmerswaal

34) _____

A. Freddie Lindstrom   B. Al Federoff

C. Jack Coffey   D. Delos Drake

35) _____

A. Eddie Robinson   B. Randy O'Neal

C. Wes Chamberlain   D. Jack Russell

36) _____

A. Roberto Duran   B. Mike Tyson

C. Richie Lewis   D. Danny Pattterson

37) _____

A. Duke Sims   B. Marv Lane

C. Reggie Sanders   D. Steve Rogers

38) _____

A. Sean Bergman   B. Roberto Hernandez

C. Bubba Trammell   D. Hal Morris

39) _____

A. Joe Cobb   B. Chet Morgan

C. Larry Yount   D. Rich Reese

40) _____

A. Virgil Trucks   B. Frank Carswell

C. Gene Packard   D. Gene Ford

41) _____

A. Roger Mason   B. Roger Weaver

C. Ed Farmer   D. Brett Butler

42) _____

A. Doug Baker   B. Bert Shepard

C. Earl Cook   D. Clyde Hatter

43) _____

A. B.J. Surhoff   B. C.J. Nitkowski

C. A.J. Sager   D. J.W. Porter

44) _____

A. Slim Love   B. Owen Friend

C. Ellis Valentine   D. Vito Valentinetti

45) _____

A. Casey Wise   B. Doug Strange

C. Curtis Pride   D. Greg Gross

46) _____

A. Kip Young   B. Jim Small

C. Bob Swift   D. Chris Short

47) _____

A. Rudy York   B. Dave Philley

C. Bun Troy   D. Daryl Boston

48) _____

A. Phil Page   B. Larry Sheets

C. Chuck Scrivener   D. Ron Reed

49) _____

A. Jose Lima   B. Billy Bean

C. Neil Berry   D. Bob Lemon

50) _____

A. Keith Moreland   B. Rich Rowland

C. Gary Sutherland   D. Toby Borland

51) _____

A. Jerry Don Gleaton   B. Andy Van Slyke

C. Andy Van Hekken   D. Todd Van Poppel

52) _____

A. Juan Acevedo   B. Benny Agbayani

C. Scott Aldred   D. Dusty Allen

53) _____

A. Paul Bako   B. Kimera Bartee

C. Milton Bradley   D. Dave Borkowski

54) _____

A. Frank Catalanotto   B. Jeff Conine

C. Enos Cabell   D. Francisco Cordero

55) _____

A. Delino DeShields   B. Jeff Datz

C. Brian Dubois   D. Mike Defelice

56) _____

A. Eric Eckenstahler   B. Joey Eischen

C. Juan Encarnacion   D. Jim Eisenreich

57) _____

A. Julio Franco   B. John Farrell

C. Scott Fletcher   D. Bob Fothergill

58) _____

A. Joe Girardi   B. Chris Gomez

C. Seth Greisinger   D. Ed Glynn

59) _____

A. Terry Harper   B. Phil Hiatt

C. Lenny Harris   D. Bill Haselman

60) _____

A. Omar Infante   B. Brandon Inge

C. Riccardo Ingram   D. Hideki Irabu

61) _____

A. Tracy Jones   B. David Justice

C. Jason Johnson   D. Marcus Jensen

62) _____

A. Dennis Kinney   B. Danny Klassen

C. Kurt Knudsen   D. Ron Kittle

63) _____

A. Mike Lansing   B. Mike Laga

C. Scott Livingstone   D. Nook Logan

64) _____

A. Jose Macias   B. Shane Mack

C. Morris Madden   D. Wendell Magee

65) _____

A. Greg Norton   B. Ron Nischwitz

C. Randy Nosek   D. Al Newman

66) _____

A. Ben Oglivie   B. Joe Oliver

C. Stubby Overmire   D. Jesse Orosco

67) _____

A. Ben Petrick   B. John Pacella

C. Dan Plesac   D. Craig Paquette

68) _____

A. Joe Randa

C. Mike Remlinger

B. Mike Rivera

D. Nate Robertson

69) _____

A. Mike Sirotka

C. Lou Sleater

B. Duane Singleton

D. Bob Sykes

70) _____

A. Gary Thurman

C. Andres Torres

B. Chris Truby

D. Ed Taubensee

71) _____

A. Tom Urbani

C. Juan Uribe

B. Jerry Ujdur

D. Ugueth Urbina

72) _____

A. Randy Veres

C. Fernando Vina

B. Pete Vuckovich

D. Tom Veryzer

73) _____

A. Gary Ward

C. Jim Walewander

B. John Wockenfuss

D. Bill Wambsganss

74) _____

A. Ernie Young

C. Kip Young

B. Dmitri Young

D. Mike Young

75) _____

A. Chris Zachary   B. Bill Zepp

C. George Zuverink   D. Richie Zisk

The 2006 Trip to the World Series

1) This Venezuelan Tiger hit the game tying home run in Game 2 of the ALDS and hit .571 for the Series to help lead the Tigers to a 3 games to 1 Series victory over the heavily favored New York Yankees?

_____

2) All of these pitchers, EXCEPT ONE, picked up a win in the ALDS vs. the Yankees. Can you find the successful series pitcher that did not garner an on paper win?

_____

A. Jamie Walker   B. Kenny Rogers

C. Joel Zumaya   D. Jeremy Bonderman

3) After only six RBIs during the regular season, this surprise Tiger DH in Game 2 of the ALCS stunned the Oakland A's by knocking in four runs which included the go-ahead two-run single, and then a sixth inning two-run home run. Can you name that Tiger?

_____

4) Which Tiger, in relief, forced a key, bases loaded, pop up in the eighth inning and pitched a solid ninth inning to pick up the win in Game 4 of the ALCS?

_____

A. Todd Jones   B. Fernando Rodney

C. Wil Ledezma   D. Jason Grilli

5) In the bottom of the ninth inning, with two outs, his second homer of Game 4, this time a three-run shot, sent the Tigers, in the most dramatic fashion, on to the World Series?

_____

6) This Tiger infielder's timely .529 hitting helped lead the Tigers to a four game sweep of the Oakland A's and won him the ALCS MVP Award?

_____

7) Although the Tigers only hit .199 as a team in the World Series, this Tiger hit a team leading .529 in the Series and also hit home runs in both Games 4 and 5?

_____

8) This Tiger hit five home runs in the playoffs including home runs in Games 1 and 2 of the World Series?

_____

9) This Tiger pitcher and his electric 23 straight scoreless innings in the post-season, led the Tigers on their charge at a 2006 World Championship. Can you name this Tiger pitcher who won a game in the ALDS, the ALCS, and then in the World Series?

_____

The Last

1) Can you name the last Tiger hitter to win the American League's Most Valuable Player?

_____

2) Can you name the last everyday Tiger to win the Rookie of the Year?

_____

3) Can you name the last Tiger to lead the American League in batting average?

_____

4) Can you name the last Tiger pitcher to lead the league in strikeouts?

_____

5) Can you name the last Tiger A.L. leader in triples?

_____

6) Who was the last Tiger to steal 50 bases? _____

7) Can you name the last Tiger to homer in old Tiger Stadium?

_____

8) Can you name the last Tiger to hit for the cycle before Carlos Guillen in 2006?

_____

9) Who was the Tigers last A.L. leader in home runs? _____

10) Who was the Tigers last A.L. leader in ERA? _____

The Answers

First Inning: Tiger Basics

Must-Knows for All Tiger Fans, the Tall and the Small …

1) Ty Cobb

2) Al Kaline

3) Mark Fidrych

4) Kirk Gibson

5) Hank Greenberg

6) Cecil Fielder

7) Mickey Lolich

8) Lou Whitaker and Alan Trammell

9) Hal Newhouser

10) Denny McLain

11) Willie Hernandez

12) Charlie Maxwell

Tiger Greats and Their Feats

13) A. Although Ty Cobb received 98 percent of the possible Hall of Fame votes, Tom Seaver, Nolan Ryan, and Cal Ripken have all received a higher percentage than Cobb.

14) C. Eddie Onslow, a Tiger in 1912, was the youngest player to hit a grand slam until Tony Conigliaro bested Onslow in 1964. A. is strange but true. Colavito took the mound for Cleveland in '58 and for New York in '68 and both games were against the Tigers.

15) D. Bunning was 20-8 with the 1957 Tigers and won 19 in his first three years with the Philadelphia Phillies, but never reached 20 wins in the National League. The A. feat is again interesting in that Bunning is the only player to accomplish this perfect feat thus far. He appeared in eight All-Star Games, having his three inning perfect appearances in the 1957 All-Star Game, and then the second perfect appearance in the second All-Star Game of the 1961 season.

16) B. Babe Ruth. Along with his 60 home run 1927 season, Ruth also had a 59 home run season in 1921.

17) D. Gehringer was a starter in the 1933 All-Star Game, but Greenberg, mostly due to his early career coinciding with the primes of Lou Gehrig and Jimmy Foxx, didn't get into an All-Star Game until 1937. Both B. and C. are interesting feats. Greenberg hit 63 doubles in 1934 and Gehringer hit 60 in 1936. Both Gehringer in '29, and Greenberg in '38, also played in 155 games in 154 game seasons.

18) C. Morris won 20 games three times, twice with the Tigers in '83 and '86, and 21 with Toronto in '92; but Morris never reached 20 wins with another team. He came closest when won 18 with Minnesota in 1991.

19) B. Sparky managed four 100-win seasons, but three times with Cincinnati and one time with Detroit. To date, no Tiger manager has ever led the Tigers to two 100-win seasons.

Up the Middle with Trammell or Whitaker and One Hodge Pudge

20) More career hits? **Whitaker** 2,369 to Trammell's 2,365.

21) More career home runs? **Whitaker** 244 to Trammell's 185.

22) Higher career batting average? **Trammell** .285 to Whitaker's .275.

23) More career stolen bases? **Trammell** 236 to Whitaker's 143.

24) More home runs in a single season **Tied** with 28 Trammell in 1987 and Whitaker in 1989.

25) Most RBIs in a single season? **Trammell** with 105 in '87 to Whitaker's 85 in '89.

26) Highest batting average in a single season? **Trammell** in 1987 with .343 to Whitaker's high in 1983 of .320.

27) Hits in a single season? **Whitaker** 206 in 1983 to Trammell's 205 in 1987.

28) **Trammell** who played 66 games for the Tigers in 1996 before retiring.

29) **A.** 19 seasons

30) **A.** Pudge was a 19-year old rookie, but future Tiger Todd Van Poppel was slightly younger than the young Pudge by a little over two months.

Second Inning: Names, Faces, Places

Nickname Match #1

1) Harry Heilmann	Slug
2) Hughie Jennings	Ee-Yah
3) Charles Hickman	Piano Legs
4) George Dauss	Hooks
5) Charlie Gehringer	The Mechanical Man
6) Aloysius Simmons	Bucketfoot Al
7) Johnny Lipon	Skids
8) Ty Cobb	The Georgia Peach
9) Herman Schaefer	Germany
10) Lynwood Rowe	Schoolboy

Nickname Match #2

11) William Donovan	Wild Bill
12) Davy Jones	Kangaroo
13) William Jacobson	Baby Doll
14) Walter Beck	Boom-Boom
15) Norman Elberfeld	The Tabasco Kid
16) John Stone	Rocky
17) Fred "Dixie" Walker	The People's Cherce
18) Ralph Works	Judge
19) Dick Bartell	Rowdy Richard
20) Bob Fothergill	Fats

Nickname Match #3

21) George Tebbetts   Birdie

22) Del Gainer   Sheriff

23) Jim Tobin   Abba Dabba

24) Paul Trout   Dizzy

25) George Winter   Sassafras

Bonus:

26) Ed Gremminger who played in 1904 with the Tigers at third base was nicknamed "Battleship" while Charley Hall who pitched six games for the Tigers in 1918 was nicknamed "Sea Lion."

Tiger Nicknames Since 1950 Match

1) Phil Regan   The Vulture

2) Frank Lary   The Yankee Killer

3) Kevin Saucier   Hot Sauce

4) Duane Sims   Duke

5) Virgil Trucks   Fire

6) Don Mossi   The Sphinx

7) Charlie Keller   King Kong

8) Mark Fidrych   The Bird

9) Earl Torgeson   The Earl of Snohomish

10) Wayne Belardi   Footsie

11) Eddie Yost   The Walking Man

12) Bob Hazle   Hurricane

13) Aurelio Lopez   Senor Smoke

14) Julio Navarro	Whiplash
15) Tom Sturdivant	Snake

From Parts Unknown

1) Barbaro Garbey	Santiago, Cuba
2) Masao Kida	Tokyo, Japan
3) Prince Oana	Waipahu, Hawaii
4) John Hiller	Toronto, Ont. Canada
5) Jason Thompson	Hollywood, California
6) Deivi Cruz	Nizao, Dominican Republic
7) Eugene Kingsale	Solito, Aruba
8) Randall Simon	Willemstad, Curacao
9) Aurelio Lopez	Tecamachalco, Mexico
10) Ivan Rodriguez	Vega Baja, Puerto Rico
11) Fritz Buelow	Berlin, Germany
12) Reno Bertoia	St. Vito Udine, Italy
13) Ben Oglivie	Colon, Panama
14) Eric Erickson	Goteborg, Sweden
15) Carlos Guillen	Maracay, Venezuela

Homegrown Products

1) Steve Gromek

2) Ted Gray

3) Art Houtteman

4) Bill Freehan

5) Tom Tresh

6) Dick "The Monster" Radatz

7) Ron LeFlore

8) Dave Rozema

9) Bill Campbell

10) Frank Tanana

11) Kirk Gibson

12) D.

13) C.

14) C.

15) B.

16) A.

Third Inning: The Great Seasons (Plus One Not-So-Great Season)

The Great Tiger Team Records

1) '61 Tigers   D. 101-61

2) '35 Tigers   G. 93-58

3) '84 Tigers   F. 104-58

4) '68 Tigers   C. 103-59

5) '72 Tigers   E. 86-70

6) '40 Tigers   B. 90-64

7) '87 Tigers   A. 98-64

8) '06 Tigers   H. 95-67

9) 1961. The famous '61 Yankees, featuring Roger Maris in his 61-home run season, put up 109 wins.

1935

1) Chicago Cubs

2) G. Goose Goslin and E. Mickey Cochrane

3) A. Schoolboy Rowe

4) C. Tommy Bridges

5) D. General Crowder

6) F. Hank Greenberg

7) B. Elden Auker

1945

1) Chicago Cubs

2) **C.** Roy Cullenbine and **F.** Rudy York

3) **B.** Eddie Mayo. Mayo had a career high with a .285 average and hit 10 of his career 26 home runs in 1945. He also had the highest fielding average for a second baseman in either league.

4) **A.** Doc Cramer

5) **E.** Virgil Trucks

6) **D.** John McHale

7) Only 1. Roy Cullenbine

Note: Hank Greenberg replaced Rudy York who was traded to pennant-winning Boston for shortstop, Eddie Lake.

Jimmy Bloodworth, a starter in 1943, returned from the War and took most of the turns at second base, although Eddie Mayo and Skeeter Webb took nearly equal time.

Newly acquired Eddie Lake took over for light-hitting Skeeter Webb.

George Kell was obtained from Philadelphia early in 1946 and hit .300 for the first time in his career in place of '45 third baseman, Bob Maier.

The '45 outfield of Cramer, Outlaw, and Cullenbine became the '46 outfield of Evers, Wakefield and Cullenbine.

Most of the catching duties were taken up by returning pre-War starter, Birdie Tebbetts.

1968

1) **D.** Mayo Smith

2) **M.** Earl Wilson

3) **H.** Dick McAuliffe

4) **C.** Pat Dobson

5) B. Don Wert

6) A. Ray Oyler

7) G. Willie Horton

8) J. Norm Cash and L. Bill Freehan

9) K. Mickey Stanley

10) F. Jim Northrup

11) I. John Hiller

12) E. Mickey Lolich

13) E. Seattle Mariners

14) C. California Angels

15) H. Baltimore Orioles

16) F. Boston Red Sox

17) A. Washington Senators

18) D. Atlanta Braves

19) G. San Diego Padres

20) B. Montreal Expos

Assembly Line 1984

Free Agents

1) Barbaro Garbey 1980

2) Juan Berenguer 1982

3, 4) Darrell Evans 1984 and Ruppert Jones 1984

Draft

5) Lance Parrish 1974

6, 7, 8) Dave Rozema, Lou Whitaker, and Tom Brookens 1975

9, 10, 11) Alan Trammell, Dan Petry, and Jack Morris 1976

12, 13) Kirk Gibson and Marty Castillo 1978

14) Howard Johnson 1979

15) Doug Baker 1982

Trades

16) 1976 Milt Wilcox from the Chicago Cubs.

17) 1978 Aurelio Lopez from St. Louis for Bob Sykes and Jack Murphy.

18) 1981 Chet Lemon from Chicago for Steve Kemp.

19) 1981 Larry Herndon from San Francisco for Dan Schatzeder and Mike Chris.

20) 1983 Doug Bair from St. Louis for Dave Rucker.

21) 1983 John Grubb from Texas for Dave Tobik.

22) 1983 Rusty Kuntz from Minnesota for Larry Pashnick.

23) 1983 Glenn Abbott from Seattle for $100,000.

24) 1984 Dave Bergman and 25) Willie Hernandez from Philadelphia for John Wockenfuss and Glenn Wilson.

26) 1984 Sid Monge from San Diego for cash.

27) 1984 Bill Scherrer from Cincinnati for Carl Willis and cash.

1984

1) Darrell Evans

2) Jack Morris

3) Glenn Abbott

4) D. Carl Willis

5) Dave Bergman

6) Marty Castillo

7) Alan Trammell

8) Lance Parrish with 33 HR

9) Kirk Gibson 27 and Chet Lemon 20

10) Milt Wilcox

11) Aurelio Lopez

12) Larry Herndon

13) Randy O' Neal

14) Doug Baker

15) Howard Johnson

16) **A.** Atlanta Braves

17) **G.** Toronto Blue Jays

18) **H.** Houston Astros

19) **C.** California Angels

20) **E.** Seattle Mariners

21) **B.** Boston Red Sox

22) **D.** Cleveland Indians

23) **I.** Texas Rangers

24) **F.** Chicago Cubs

And One Not-So-Great Season, 2003

1) **B.** Dmitri Young

2) **E.** Alex Sanchez

3) **A.** Craig Monroe

4) **C.** Mike Maroth, with 9 wins.

5) **D.** Steve Avery 2-0

6) D. 5

7) B. Ramon Santiago, who led the league with 18 sacrifice hits.

8) C. Four pitchers made their major league debut in the same game. Jeremy Bonderman went 4 innings, Wil Ledezma, 2, Chris Spurling, 1, and Matt Roney, 1.

9) C. Young had two home runs, two triples, and a single, to total 15 bases in a single game, one total base behind the Tiger record set by Ty Cobb in 1925.

10) D. Brandon Inge

Fourth Inning: Go Get 'em Tigers

Thanks for Stopping By: Tigers' Genius Edition

1) Jack Coombs

2) Wally Schang

3) Al Simmons

4) Babe Herman

5) Earl Averill

6) Hank Borowy

7) Gene Bearden

8) Johnny Hopp

9) Ferris Fain

10) Larry Doby

11) Sandy Amoros

12) Johnny Podres

13) Mike Marshall

14) Roy Face

15) Dean Chance

16) Alex Johnson

17) Elias Sosa

18) Dave Collins

19) Bill Madlock

20) Hideo Nomo

21) Luis Gonzalez

22) Francisco Cordero

23) Steve Avery

Unlucky Seven

1) B. Eric Davis

2) A. Fred Lynn

3) E. Ruben Sierra

4) D. Gregg Jefferies

5) G. Juan Gonzalez

6) F. Juan Samuel

7) C. Vince Coleman

You Were a Tiger?

1) Wally Pipp

2) Howard Ehmke

3) Rip Sewell

4) Earl Webb

5) Billy Pierce

6) Johnny Pesky

7) Vic Wertz

8) Walt Dropo

9) Gus Zernial

10) Phil Regan

11) Eddie Mathews

12) Frank Howard

13) Jim Slaton

14) Jack Billingham

15) David Wells

Fifth Inning: The Good Old Days

The Good Old Days, 1901-1950

1) Bennett Park

2) Milwaukee Brewers

3) C. 1905

4) D. 1904 The Tigers wore the Old English "D" on their road uniforms for the first time during the '04 season. In 1905, the traditional Tigers' "D" first appeared on the home whites.

5) D. Play in 162 games. Although the American League had only a 154 game schedule, the Tigers tied ten times in 1904 and replayed eight of those games making Barrett the first to play in 162 regular season games, the current number of games on the major league schedule.

6) B. Bobby Lowe

7) B. Sam Thompson

8) 1907

9) Triples, with an amazing career mark of 312. But, if you said inside-the-park home runs, you would also be correct. Crawford had 51 for his career.

10) C. Lead both the N.L. and A.L. in home runs. Crawford led the N.L. with 16 while with Cincinnati in 1901, and led the A.L. by belting 7 round trippers with the Tigers in 1908.

11) The Chicago Cubs, winning the 1907 and 1908 N.L. pennants with their famed infield of Tinker, Evers, Chance and their forgotten third baseman, Harry Steinfeldt.

12) D. 9. In fact, Cobb's league leading 9 home runs were all inside-the-park home runs. He was the only player in the 20th century to lead the league in home runs without hitting a single home run out of the park. Cobb also led the A.L. in stolen bases making him the only player ever to win this quadruple crown.

13) Pittsburgh Pirates

14) Hughie Jennings

15) **B.** Del Pratt

16) George Mullin, a 7-0 victory against the St. Louis Browns.

17) **A.** Harry Coveleski

18) **C.** Jack Quinn

Explanation: Ayers and Leonard were both Tigers when the spitball was legalized. Mitchell pitched five games for the Tigers in 1911, resurfaced with Cincinnati in 1916, and pitched until he was 41. Incidentally, Mitchell was also the batter who lined into the World Series unassisted triple play turned by Bill Wambsganss in the 1920 World Series. The answer is **C.** Jack Quinn, who pitched in four decades in the major leagues, but never pitched for the Tigers during his 23 major league seasons.

19) Harry Heilmann

20) **C.** 5

21) George "Hooks" Dauss

22) **B.** John Stone

23) Firpo Marberry

24) Tommy Bridges

25) Mickey Cochrane

26) **B.** Marv Owen

27) **True,** Gehringer played in 511 straight games from Sept. 3rd, 1927, through May 7th, 1931, and then put up a 504 consecutive game streak from June 25th, 1932, through August 11th, 1935.

28) **A.** Only four regular second basemen had enough chances to qualify and all made 25 errors. Gehringer, of course, having more chances, led the league in fielding percentage while also leading the league in errors.

29) **C.** Gee Walker

30) **B.** Pete Fox

31) **B.** 44 in 1946, his last season as a Tiger. Greenberg hit over 40 home runs four times during his twelve seasons in a Tiger uniform.

32) Bobo Newsom

33) Dizzy Trout

34) True

35) **A.** Johnny Groth

36) George Kell

The Good Old Days, 1951-2006

37) **A.** Kell and **C.** Wertz homered at home in the '51 contest. Doby got just one at bat in the '51 All-Star Game representing Cleveland, but would later homer for Cleveland when Cleveland hosted the Mid-Summer Classic in 1954. Howard was still seven years away from being a big leaguer in 1951, but in 1969, he joined Kell, Wertz, and Doby as players who had hit a home run in their home park in an All-Star Game when he homered as a Washington Senator at R.F.K. Stadium.

38) Fred Hutchinson

39) Virgil Trucks

40) Al Kaline

41) **D.** Gail Harris

42) **C.** 7

43) **A.** Steve Demeter

44) **A.** The slanted script Tigers, in the Dodgers' style, on the 1960 home whites. Our Old "D" was returned in 1961.

45) Bill Bruton

46) Rocky Colavito

47) Dick McAuliffe 1960

48) Bill Freehan 1961

49) Willie Horton 1963

50) Jim Northrup 1964

51) Hank Aguirre

52) Jerry Lumpe

53) The Tigers were no-hit by Baltimore's Steve Barber and Stu Miller, but managed to eke out the 2-1 win.

54) and 55) Mickey Lolich and Joe Coleman

56) **False.** The Tigers won the division by a ½ game after clinching the East on Oct. 3rd and losing Oct. 4th against Boston in the strike-shortened season.

57) **A.** Woodie Fryman

58) Oakland A's

59) Gates Brown

60) **C.** 38 Saves in '73 and 17 Wins in '74.

61) **A.** Colbert hit 5 home runs and drove in 13 runs in one day.

62) **A.** Rusty Staub, 101 RBIs, and Jason Thompson, 105 RBIs.

63) Richie Hebner

64) **A.** Most Home Runs in a season by an A.L. catcher.

65) **C.** Triples

66) Milt Wilcox

67) **True.** Jack Morris led the '84 Tigers with 19 wins.

68) **C.** Hit home runs from both sides of the plate in one game.

69) **B.** 38

70) Darnell Coles

71) **False.** Gibson never played in an All-Star Game.

72) Mark Thurmond

73) Doyle Alexander

74) **True**

75) Pat Sheridan

76) Minnesota Twins

77) **B.** Dave Palmer

78) Lloyd Moseby

79) Tony Phillips

80) **C.** Lou Whitaker

81) New Comiskey Park, currently known as U.S. Cellular Field.

82) Bill Gullickson

83) Dan Gladden

84) **B.** Hit for the Cycle

85) **D.** Brad Ausmus

86) **B.** Chad Curtis

87) Gregg Olson

88) Bob Hamelin

89) Brian Hunter

90) **A.** Sean Runyan

91) **B.** David Wells '95

92) **E.** Travis Fryman '96

93) **C.** Justin Thompson '97

94) **A.** Damion Easley '98

95) **D.** Brad Ausmus '99

96) 3rd **Team:** Texas, Kansas City, Detroit

97) Brian Moehler. The last game at Tiger Stadium Sept. 27th, 1999, against K.C. and the first game at Comerica Park on April 11th, 2000, against Seattle.

98) Seattle Mariners

99) Todd Jones

100) Shane Halter

101) **B.** Get 6 hits in a nine inning game.

102) **A.** George Lombard and Wendell Magee

103) Rob Fick

104) **True.** 106 losses in 2002 and 119 losses in 2003.

105) **D.** Carlos Pena

106) Carlos Guillen

107) **D.** Brandon Inge

108) Sean Casey

Sixth Inning: Bless You Boys

Rookie Years: The Hard Ones

1) D. Ed Summers

2) B. Sammy Hale

3) E. Dale Alexander

4) C. Barney McCosky

5) F. Dick Wakefield

6) A. Chuck Hostetler

7) G. Pat Mullin

Rookie Years: The Bit Easier Ones

8) A. Rudy York

9) F. Harvey Kuenn

10) D. Jake Wood

11) C. Dave Rozema

12) G. Glenn Wilson

13) I. Eric King

14) E. Mike Henneman

15) B. Matt Nokes

16) H. Tony Clark

It's All Relative

1) Delahanty

2) Coveleski

3) Sullivan

4) Manush

5) Trout

6) Kell

7) Kennedy

8) Boone

9) Virgil

10) Sisler

11) Sherry

12) Perry

13) Niekro

14) Coleman

15) Nettles

16) Underwood

17) Mahler

18) Weaver

19) **C.** Father, Jack Lively with Detroit in 1911, and son, Bud Lively with Cincinnati in 1947.

20) Billy Ripken

21) **D.** Frank and Milt Bolling and they played together with the Tigers in 1958.

22) Nate Cornejo

23) **B.** Steve and Jason Grilli

24) Jeff and Kyle Farnsworth

25) Cecil Fielder

26) Delmon Young

Managerial Insight

1) George Stallings

2) Ed Barrow

3) George Moriarty

4) Del Baker

5) Steve O'Neill

6) Red Rolfe

7) Fred Hutchinson

8) Bucky Harris

9) Jimmie Dykes

10) Joe Gordon

11) Billy Martin

12) Joe Schultz

13) Ralph Houk

14) Buddy Bell

15) Larry Parrish

16) Phil Garner

17) Steve Boros

18) Jackie Moore

19) Larry Doby

20) Frank Howard

21) Johnny Lipon

22) Eddie Mathews

23) Johnny Pesky

24) Birdie Tebbetts

25) Harvey Kuenn

26) Gene Lamont

27) Bruce Kimm

28) Ray Knight

29) Jerry Manuel

30) Bob Melvin

31) Al Pedrique

32) Whitey Herzog

Seventh Inning: The Good, The-Not-So Good, The Bad, The Sometimes Ugly, and The Oh So Obscure

The 1912 Replacement Game

1) D. Deacon McGuire

2) C. Aloysius Travers

3) B. Ed Irvin

4) A. Joe Sugden

5) E. Billy Maharg

6) D. Dan McGarvey

The 1919 Black Sox

1) Kid Gleason

2) Eddie Cicotte

3) Billy Maharg, his playing name. His given surname was Graham, which, for baseball, he spelled backwards, giving it that more sinister/conspiratorial feel.

4) Lefty Williams

5) Fred McMullin

6) "Sleepy" Bill Burns

7) Grover "Slim" Lowdermilk

8) Jean "Chauncey" Dubuc

The '27 Tigers: Genius Addition

1) Harry Heilmann

2) Charlie Gehringer

3) **True.** But only three of them finished with a better than .500 record.

Here is the breakdown:

Earl Whitehill was 16-14

Lil Stoner was 10-13

Sam Gibson was 11-12

Ken Holloway was 11-12

Rip Collins was 13-7

Ownie Carroll was 10-6

4) Johnny Neun

5) Bob Fothergill

6) D. Stolen Bases with 141. The Tigers' league-leading total was 51 more than the slugging Yankees and eight more than Washington, who finished in third place in the A.L. in '27.

7) Mark Koenig 1930-'31, Waite Hoyt '30-'31, Joe Dugan 1931, Johnny Grabowski 1931

Special K'ers

1) D. Pete Incaviglia

2) A. Rob Deer

3) B. Cecil Fielder

4) E. Dean Palmer

5) C. Travis Fryman

6) B. Bobby Higginson

In the L Column

1) A. Mike Maroth

2) E. Doyle Alexander

3) D. Brian Moehler

4) C. Mike Moore

5) B. Tim Belcher

The Obscure

1) A. Oscar Stanage

2) C. Johnny Bassler

3) A. Chief Hogsett

4) A. Fred Gladding

5) B. Gus Triandos

6) C. Lerrin LaGrow

7) B. Mick Kelleher

8) C. Dave Tobik

9) C. Dickie Noles

10) D. Don Heinkel

11) A. Omar Olivares

12) True

13) True

14) True

15) True

16) True

17) B. Ed Farmer/Al Cowens

18) B. Alejandro Sanchez

19) B. Chet Lemon

20) C. Mel Rojas had a 22.74 ERA in 1999.

Seventh Inning Stretch ... Take Me Out to the Ballgame

First Basemen

1) Dale Alexander	Right
2) Hank Greenberg	Right
3) Rudy York	Right
4) Norm Cash	Left
5) Jason Thompson	Left
6) Enos Cabell	Right
7) Darrell Evans	Left
8) Cecil Fielder	Right
9) Tony Clark	Both
10) Dmitri Young	Both
11) Carlos Pena	Left
12) Chris Shelton	Right

Second Basemen

13) Germany Schaefer	Right
14) Charlie Gehringer	Left
15) Gerry Priddy	Right
16) Frank Bolling	Right
17) Jake Wood	Right
18) Dick McAuliffe	Left
19) Lou Whitaker	Left

20) Tony Phillips	Both
21) Damion Easley	Right
22) Fernando Vina	Left
23) Placido Polanco	Right

Shortstops

24) Donie Bush	Both
25) Billy Rogell	Both
26) Johnny Lipon	Right
27) Harvey Kuenn	Right
28) Chico Fernandez	Right
29) Ed Brinkman	Right
30) Alan Trammell	Right
31) Deivi Cruz	Right
32) Shane Halter	Right
33) Omar Infante	Right
34) Carlos Guillen	Both

Third Basemen

35) Marv Owen	Right
36) George Kell	Right
37) Ray Boone	Right
38) Don Wert	Right
39) Aurelio Rodriguez	Right
40) Tom Brookens	Right

41) Howard Johnson   Both

42) Travis Fryman   Right

43) Dean Palmer   Right

44) Eric Munson   Left

45) Brandon Inge   Right

Catchers

46) Charles Schmidt   Both

47) Oscar Stanage   Right

48) Johnny Bassler   Left

49) Mickey Cochrane   Left

50) Birdie Tebbetts   Right

51) Bob Swift   Right

52) Bill Freehan   Right

53) Milt May   Left

54) Lance Parrish   Right

55) Matt Nokes   Left

56) Mickey Tettleton   Both

57) Brad Ausmus   Right

58) Ivan Rodriguez   Right

59) Vance Wilson   Right

Outfielders

Early Days

60) Sam Crawford	Left
61) Ty Cobb	Left
62) Bobby Veach	Left
63) Harry Heilmann	Right
64) Heinie Manush	Left
65) Bob Fothergill	Right
66) Gee Walker	Right
67) Goose Goslin	Left

Middle Ages

68) Hoot Evers	Right
69) Vic Wertz	Left
70) Al Kaline	Right
71) Charlie Maxwell	Left
72) Rocky Colavito	Right
73) Bill Bruton	Left
74) Don Demeter	Right
75) Willie Horton	Right
76) Mickey Stanley	Right
77) Jim Northrup	Left
78) Ron LeFlore	Right
79) Steve Kemp	Left

Modern Age

80) Kirk Gibson	Left
81) Larry Herndon	Right
82) Chet Lemon	Right
83) Gary Pettis	Both
84) Fred Lynn	Left
85) Dan Gladden	Right
86) Rob Deer	Right
87) Bobby Higginson	Left
88) Juan Encarnacion	Right
89) Rondell White	Right
90) Nook Logan	Both
91) Curtis Granderson	Left
92) Craig Monroe	Right
93) Marcus Thames	Right
94) Magglio Ordonez	Right

Pitchers

95) Frank Tanana	Left
96) Jack Morris	Right
97) Willie Hernandez	Left
98) Denny McLain	Right
99) Mickey Lolich	Left
100) John Hiller	Left
101) Hal Newhouser	Left

102) Tommy Bridges	Right
103) "Hooks" Dauss	Right
104) Schoolboy Rowe	Right
105) Jim Bunning	Right
106) Aurelio Lopez	Right
107) Todd Jones	Right
108) Jeff Weaver	Right
109) Mike Maroth	Left
110) Jeremy Bonderman	Right
111) Kenny Rogers	Left
112) Justin Verlander	Right
113) Fernando Rodney	Right
114) Nate Robertson	Left
115) Joel Zumaya	Right

With the First Pick …

1) Mike Ivie	1970 San Diego Padres
2) Mike Moore	1981 Seattle Mariners
3) Tim Belcher	1983 Minnesota Twins
4) Phil Nevin	1992 Houston Astros
5) Matt Anderson	1997 Detroit Tigers

Bean or Beane?

1) Beane

2) Bean

3) Bean

4) Bean .226 to Beane's .219.

5) Beane

The Last Game at Tiger Stadium

1) 11

2) 6

3) 2

4) 21

5) 3

6) 47

7) 5

8) Because Kapler was representing Ty Cobb, and in Cobb's day there were not yet numbers on the uniform, Kapler had no number on the back of his jersey.

9) Norm Cash

10) Jones was wearing his own, #59.

Eighth Inning: Hodge Podge and Such

The Hodge and the Podge

1) Jim Curry

2) Earl Whitehill

3) Darrell Evans

4) Charlie Gehringer

5) Ralph Branca

6) Floyd Giebell

7) Gates Brown

8) Rocky Colavito

9) Al Benton

10) Dick Tracewski

11) Norm Cash

12) Jim Bunning

13) Schoolboy Rowe

14) Ike Brown

15) Cesar Gutierrez

16) Bob Cain

17) Jim Delsing

18) Paul Foytack

19) Doug Flynn

20) Rusty Staub

21) Phil Mankowski

22) Bill Fahey

23) Duffy Dyer

24) Jack Billingham

25) John Mohardt

26) Ken Williams

27) Rick Leach

Trade Bait

1) Doyle Alexander

2) Dick Littlefield

3) Dave Engle

4) Ownie Carroll

5) Denny McLain

6) Tuck Stainback

7) Harvey Kuenn

8) Barney McCosky

9) Steve Demeter

10) Dave LaPoint

11) Brad Ausmus

12) Frank Catalanotto

13) Juan Encarnacion

14) Jeff Weaver

15) Kyle Farnsworth

Simply Golden Gloves

1) Frank Lary

2) C. 1968. He then spent the World Series playing shortstop.

3) Bill Freehan

4) Ed Brinkman

5) C. Aurelio Rodriguez

6) **A.** Alan Trammell won the first of his four Gold Gloves in 1980. Lou Whitaker the first of his three consecutive Gold Gloves in 1983. Lance Parrish also won the first of his Gold Gloves in 1983 and had the same run of three consecutive Gold Gloves as Lou Whitaker. Jack Morris never won a Gold Glove.

7) Dwayne Murphy

8) Gary Pettis, 1989

Ninth inning: In For the Save

Over The Roof

1) Norm Cash

2) Kirk Gibson

3) Cecil Fielder

4) Ruppert Jones on June 24th, 1984, against Milwaukee.

5) **C.** Jim Northrup

6) **B.** Willie Horton

7) **A.** Karim Garcia

The Rest of the Story

1915 For the first time in their history, the Tigers won 100 games, but were beaten out by 2 ½ games by the Bostons who had a young lefty in his first full season named Ruth. The Tigers' offense was led by the outfield where **TY COBB** hit .369, to lead the league, and also set an American League record with 96 stolen bases that stood until 1980. **SAM CRAWFORD** and **BOBBY VEACH** tied for the A.L lead in RBIs with 112. **HARRY COVELESKI** pitched 50 games winning 22, and **HOOKS DAUSS** won 24 games en route to becoming the all-time Tigers' leader in wins.

1923 Under the leadership of player-manager Ty Cobb, the Tigers finished a distant second, 16 games behind the New York Yankees. The Tigers hit .300 as a team, but that was only the league's second-best team average with third place Cleveland hitting .301. **HARRY HEILMANN** led the offense putting up a .403 average and was the last Tiger to hit .400 for a season. He also added 18 home runs which was good for third behind Babe Ruth, and Ken Williams of the St. Louis Browns. Manager, Cobb, hit .340 and seven regulars hit over .300. The pitching staff was led by Hooks Dauss and his 21 wins, the last of his three 20-win seasons. The Tigers also had the league leader in losses, **HERM PIL-LETTE,** who went 14-19 this year after a 19-12 rookie year in 1922.

1937 On May 25th, player-manager **MICKEY COCHRANE** was accidentally hit in the head by a pitched ball which prematurely ended his Hall of Fame playing career. Despite the loss of their manager, the Tigers went on to win 89 games, finishing a distant second to the New York Yankees. Sporting the second highest A.L. team ERA of 4.87, the Tigers won with their strength at bat, hitting .292 as a team to lead the American League. **HANK GREENBERG** put up his 183 RBI season this year good for the third highest single season total of all time. Second baseman, **CHARLIE GEHRINGER,** led the league with a .371 average and won the A.L. MVP. **RUDY YORK** added 35 home runs in his rookie season and hit 18 in August alone to break Babe Ruth's record for home runs in a single month. The MVP second baseman, the shortstop **BILLY ROGELL**, and third baseman **MARV OWEN,** all led the A.L. in fielding at their positions. The Tigers were led in wins by **ROXIE LAWSON** who put up an 18-7 record, despite a 5.26 ERA, and by **ELDEN AUKER,** who added 17 wins with a team-leading 3.88 ERA.

1967 In one of the most memorable pennant races to date, four teams, Detroit, Chicago, Boston, and Minnesota, were vying for the pennant, going into the final weekend of the season. The Tigers, forced by weather into two double-headers against the California Angels on the last two days of the season, needed to sweep all four games to assure themselves a trip to the World Series. But, with a depleted pitching staff, the Tigers were only able to manage two wins in those final four games and finished at 91 wins, tying the Tigers for second place in the four-way pennant race. The Tigers strong pitching staff was led by **EARL WILSON** and his A.L. leading 22 wins. Their team batting average was a mere .243, but in the pitcher-friendly era, was good enough for second in the league. **AL KALINE** led the way on offense with his .308 average which placed him third in the A.L. and his 25 home runs which tied him for the fourth high-est total in the A.L. for the '67 season.

1981 The Tigers finished the season with the second most wins in the A.L and went into the last weekend of the season with a chance to make the divisional playoffs as the second half A.L. East champions of the strike-shortened split season. But, our youthful Tigers were unable to win the necessary two out of three games and instead watched the Milwaukee Brewers celebrate. The team leader in home runs, **LANCE PARRISH,** had a mere 10. **STEVE KEMP** led the team with 49 RBIs and was traded after the season for longtime Tiger center fielder Chet Lemon. The team leader in wins, **JACK MORRIS,** had 14 which was good enough to tie for the A.L. lead with three other pitchers. Second year outfielder, **KIRK GIBSON,** led the second half charge batting .328 for the season.

1988 Although the Tigers led the A.L. East longer than any other division rival, a late season 4-19 swoon led to a second place finish one game behind Boston. **ALAN TRAMMELL** led the team with a .311 average and also led the team with 69 RBIs. **DARRELL EVANS** hit 22 home runs to lead the club and also hit his 400th career home run in this, his last Tiger season. Newly acquired outfielder **GARY PETTIS** played Gold Glove center field and, despite hitting only .210 for the season, stole 44 bases to finish second in bases stolen in the A.L. Jack Morris led the staff with 15 wins and a surprising, second year Tiger, **JEFF ROBINSON,** started 23 games going 13-6, and allowed the least hits per nine innings in Tiger history. Another second year Tiger, **MIKE HENNEMAN,** had a spectacular year out of the pen, winning 9 games and saving 22, with a 1.87 ERA.

1993 In what would be the last winning season at Tiger Stadium, the Tigers resided in first place until June, but finished in fourth place in the A.L. East with a record of 85-77. The team scored the most runs in the American League and hit the second most home runs, but the free-swinging offense also led the A.L. in strikeouts. The offensive attack was led by **CECIL FIELDER** with his 30 homers and his 117 RBIs, good for fifth in the A.L. after he had led the junior circuit in RBIs for three straight seasons. **MICKEY TETTLETON** led the team in home runs with 32. **JOHN DOHERTY** led the struggling, high ERA pitching staff with 14 wins, and Mike Henneman led the Tigers out of the pen with 24 saves.

Four For 2004

1) Carlos Pena

2) Carlos Guillen

3) Nate Robertson

4) Ugueth Urbina

Five For 2005

1) Magglio Ordonez

2) Troy Percival

3) Dmitri Young

4) Ivan Rodriguez

5) Placido Polanco

Six For 2006

1) Kenny Rogers

2) Todd Jones

3) Chris Shelton

4) Justin Verlander

5) Jim Leyland

6) C. Carlos Guillen

Tenth Inning: Extra Innings

One of These Things …

1) C. Neal Ball

2) D. Jack Spring

3) D. Phil Roof

4) D. Mickey Rivers

5) C. Chico Salmon

6) C. Doug Bird

7) C. Les Moss, although he was a Tiger manger in 1979.

8) A. Joe Black

9) A. Ollie Brown

10) B. Frank White

11) D. Larry French

12) A. Mel Queen, neither of the two MLB Mel Queens played for the Tigers.

13) B. Don Money

14) C. Charlie Silvera

15) C. Dave Cash

16) D. Nippy Jones

17) B. Travis Jackson, one of the least well known HOFs, inducted, 1982.

18) C. Dave Smith

19) D. Reggie Cleveland

20) A. Joe Bush

21) B. Otis Nixon

22) D. Alex Burr

23) **B.** Mudcat Grant

24) **B.** Dan Ford

25) **A.** Ed Hemingway

26) **C.** Buck Freeman, neither MLB Buck Freeman played for the Tigers.

27) **C.** Bobby Brown, neither MLB Bobby Brown played for the Tigers.

28) **C.** Jose Pagan

29) **A.** Razor Shines

30) **D.** Dick Allen

31) **C.** Bill Lee, neither Bill Lee, both of whom were All-Stars, were ever Tigers.

32) **B.** Doug Gwosdz, nicknamed "Eye Chart."

33) **D.** Win Remmerswaal

34) **A.** Freddie Lindstrom, inducted into the Hall of Fame in 1976.

35) **C.** Wes Chamberlain

36) **B.** Mike Tyson

37) **D.** Steve Rogers

38) **B.** Roberto Hernandez

39) **C.** Larry Yount

40) **C.** Gene Packard

41) **D.** Brett Butler

42) **B.** Bert Shepard

43) **A.** B.J. Surhoff

44) **C.** Ellis Valentine

45) **D.** Greg Gross

46) **D.** Chris Short

47) **D.** Daryl Boston

48) **D.** Ron Reed

49) **D.** Bob Lemon, inducted into the Hall of Fame in 1976.

50) **D.** Toby Borland

51) **B.** Andy Van Slyke

52) **B.** Benny Agbayani

53) **C.** Milton Bradley

54) **B.** Jeff Conine

55) **A.** Delino DeShields

56) **D.** Jim Eisenreich

57) **A.** Julio Franco

58) **A.** Joe Girardi

59) **C.** Lenny Harris

60) **D.** Hideki Irabu

61) **B.** David Justice

62) **D.** Ron Kittle

63) **A.** Mike Lansing

64) **B.** Shane Mack

65) **D.** Al Newman

66) **D.** Jesse Orosco

67) **C.** Dan Plesac

68) **C.** Mike Remlinger

69) **A.** Mike Sirotka

70) **D.** Ed Taubensee

71) **C.** Juan Uribe

72) **B.** Pete Vuckovich

73) **D.** Bill Wambsganss

74) **D.** Mike Young

75) D. Richie Zisk

The 2006 Trip to the World Series

1) Carlos Guillen

2) C. Joel Zumaya, although his 100 mph plus fastballs and three strikeout, dominating performance against the Yankees gave the Tigers a huge psychological lift on their way to their 3-1 ALDS victory.

3) Alexis Gomez

4) C. Wil Ledezma

5) Magglio Ordonez

6) Placido Polanco

7) Sean Casey

8) Craig Monroe

9) Kenny Rogers

The Last

1) Hank Greenberg, all the way back in 1940. The Tigers had three different hitters win the MVP Award in the '30s, with Mickey Cochrane in 1934, Hank Greenberg in 1935, and Charlie Gehringer in 1937, but the Tigers have not had a hitter win the MVP award since Greenberg won the MVP in 1940.

2) Lou Whitaker, in 1978

3) Norm Cash, hit .361 in 1961. Cash put up one of baseball's great statistical fluke seasons, his next highest average being .286 in 1960.

4) Jack Morris, in 1983, with 232 strikeouts.

5) Jake Wood, 1961

6) Roger Cedeno, with 55 steals in 2001.

7) Rob Fick

8) Damion Easley, on June 8th, 2001, in a 9-4 win against the Milwaukee Brewers.

9) Cecil Fielder, with 44 home runs in 1991, to tie Jose Canseco for the A.L. lead.

10) Mark Fidrych, with a 2.34 ERA, in his rookie year.

Bibliography

Great Tiger Books of Help:

Hawkins, John C. *This Date in Detroit Tigers History.* NY: Stein and Day, 1981.

Hawkins, Jim. et all. *The Detroit Tigers Encyclopedia.* Champaign, IL: Sports Publishing, 2003.

Great Baseball Books of Help:

Forker, Dom. *The Ultimate Baseball Quiz Book.* NY: A Signet Book, 1988.

Reichler, Joseph L. *Baseball Encyclopedia.* NY: Thomson Gale, 1988.

Neft, David S. et all. *The Sports Encyclopedia: Baseball 2004.* NY: St. Martin's Press, 2004.

Nemec, David. *Great Baseball Feats, Facts, & Firsts.* NY: A Signet Book, 1990.

Shatzkin, Mike. Ed. *The Ballplayers.* NY: The Idea Logical Press, 1990.

Great Web Sites of Help:

Baseball Reference.com
> http://www.baseball-reference.com

Baseball Almanac.com
> http://www.baseball-almanac.com

Baseball Library.com
> http://www.baseballlibrary.com

MLB com.
> http://mlb.mlb.com

Tigers Central.com
> http://www.tigerscentral.com

About the Author

Eric J. Pierzchala was born and raised in Detroit, Michigan and grew up playing baseball in the greater Detroit area. After graduating from Harper Woods Notre Dame in Harper Woods, Michigan, Eric completed his undergraduate work at Kent State University and is a current graduate student at The University of Akron. Along with working on his literary career, Pierzchala has pursued a number of diverse activities which included a stint in professional baseball as one of the very few professional knuckleball pitchers.

978-0-595-42035-3
0-595-42035-4

Printed in the United States
75600LV00005B/172-174